LIBER

A Life in the Service of Christ and His Church

The Story of Ed Kofi, a Liberian missionary, and the church he
founded, African Christian Fellowship International (**ACFI**)

By
Joan Brown

Creative Force Press

Creative Force Press

Liberian Son
© 2016 by Joan Brown
www.acfiliberia.org

This title is also available as an eBook. Visit
www.CreativeForcePress.com/titles for more information.

Published by Creative Force Press
4704 Pacific Ave, Suite C, Lacey, WA 98503
www.CreativeForcePress.com

ISBN: 978-1-939989-25-3

Cover art by Joan Brown
Printed in the United States of America

Disclaimer

The views and opinions expressed in this book are those of the author's and do not reflect the views and positions of the authors of the sources cited in this work. We are grateful for author Nicolai Lidow who embarked upon the massive undertaking of careful research and study of the Liberian civil war from the philosophical point of view. The information drawn from his careful research was meant to give you, the reader, some background of the warring factions and phases of the war. It is my hope that Lidow's excellent, careful analysis of the rebel factions will inform others who study warfare to better understand such complex civil wars and assist in diffusing them quicker, ultimately thwarting the atrocities committed against civilian populations.

"It has been my honour to have known and worked alongside Edward Kofi, his wife Cecelia and ACFI for 25 years. During those years, Edward and his wife have led as servants; leading with influence and godly wisdom from the halls of government to the widows and orphans in war-torn nations. As is true of most effective Christian leaders, Edward and his family have experienced profound success and miraculous works of God, along with hardship and intense pain. ACFI under Edward's leadership has made a lasting impact to the glory of God in the lives of so many in sub-Sahara West Africa as well as partners in North America and Europe."
—Wayne Shenk, Elder – Northside Church, British Columbia

"After more than 20 years traveling to Liberia and experiencing firsthand so many of the things you read in this book, I have to pinch myself when I reflect on how God has done so much with people who have so little. But then I remind myself that my ACFI friends have enormous faith, unquenchable joy and unearthly courage. I have never been around Ed Kofi and the many African men and women who count me their brother without feeling like I'm the small one. They continue to school my soul."
—Bruce Stabbert, Pastor – Fellowship Bible Church, Tacoma, WA

To Ed and Cece

As for me, I shall call upon God,
And the LORD will save me.
Psalm 55:16

Contents

Preface

Inside this small volume is a large story. It's a story of Christ's love for the nations expressed in His providential raising up of an indigenous ministry from a squalid slum in West Africa. In a day when beleaguered North American Christians are more and more turning inward to survive the battle for the Bible and for souls on the local front, we must constantly force ourselves to remember that the war for Christ's Gospel has always been international in scope, as international as Acts 1:8 has always made it ("the remotest part of the earth"). This would not matter—who could blame us for tending our own orchards or bandaging our own wounded?—except that the supremacy of Christ is ever and always for all peoples and nations. Frankly, if we neglect to constantly fan that world-wide passion and attach prayers, feet and dollars to our heart, then we will soon find that local efforts to pursue the honor of Christ's name echo hollow with a simple lie: that God could be proclaimed King but not the King of all nations. We could not wholeheartedly join with the psalmist: "Sing praises to our King...for God is the King of all the earth" (Psalm 46).

As you read the following chapters, realize that for decades God has been intimately involved in the lives of far-off people who you've never thought about as you go about your daily life. However, many North American Christians have had the life-changing honor of partnering with these courageous, faithful people and watching their stories unfold. It is a large story because it is the story of a large God. Our prayer is simply that this record of God's involvement in West Africa will ignite in you a desire to help.

Bruce Stabbert

The Tie-Tie Vine

The Tie-Tie is a vine the Liberians harvest from a tree of the same name. It is in high demand in rural villages, used to create shelter, strong baskets and traps for fish. Acquiring enough can be a challenge. Through great labor and time spent, there can be a harvest of Tie-Tie.

Ed Kofi, founder of the church, African Christian Fellowship International, asks, *what if an elephant snagged his foot on the vine still attached to the tree?* Because of his sheer size and power, every movement would harvest more and more rope, even seemingly small movements. What a few men would take much time to gather, an elephant could gather quickly.

What if the vine were the Lord's harvest of souls in West Africa, those souls to whom Ed Kofi has devoted his life to bringing the Gospel? What if the global Church were the elephant? Every faithful shepherd has a heart that is breaking as he or she contemplates the lost souls God has placed within his or her midst. Ed is no different. His hands have bled from gripping the vine. His back has felt as though it would break for the strain of the pull.

According to Revelation 7, people of every nation, tribe and tongue will stand together before the throne of God, singing praises to Him and to the Lamb. We will see the faces of West Africans engaged in rapturous worship, and I wonder if we will feel a sense of *I could have done more.* I wonder if we will have a flash of a moment of our time on the earth when we could have joined our brothers and sisters, placed our hands on the vine beneath theirs, and pulled. Will we have that awareness in heaven as we stand with them and sing?

Introduction

In journeys often, in perils of waters,
in perils of robbers, in perils of my own countrymen,
in perils of the Gentiles, in perils in the city,
in perils in the wilderness, in perils in the sea,
in perils among false brethren;
in weariness and toil, in sleeplessness often,
in hunger and in thirst, in fastings often,
in cold and nakedness.
Besides other things, what comes upon me daily:
my deep concern for all the churches.
(2 Corinthians 11:26-28)

What burdens have you gathered along the way and carry upon your shoulders? What load do you bear as you walk the earth? If you could be relieved of your load, would you pass it to another? When the load is too heavy for the strength of your thighs, do you collapse under its weight and curse the One who entrusted it to you?

I know a man who carries a people. I know a man who carries a nation. And what he tells me is that the LORD God Almighty is the strength of his thighs, that these are His people, that this is His nation. I am writing of a Liberian man named Tshainfuer Edward Kofi, and of his homeland, Liberia, and more beloved, his countrymen and women. This is the story of his lifework as a true bondservant of the Most High God. And he would have me tell you from the beginning of this book that

13

it is Jesus Christ to whom all honor belongs for the miraculous wonders and salvation of souls Edward has been so blessed to witness. Come alongside him, read of his calling, his church planting, and his Lord, Who, while seated at His throne in heaven, is present on earth intervening in the activities of the saints and supplying their needs.

1

A Brief History of Liberia and Ed's Childhood

Tshainfuer Edward Kofi (Ed) was born in 1954 in the village of Pynetown (Tarsue) Sinoe County in southern Liberia on the west coast of the African continent. He is of the Kru tribe of Tarsue which is a section of the Kru tribe in Sinoe County. He is one of ten children.

In the United States of America, during the 1700's and 1800's there were many points of view as to how to manage the growing population of freed slaves. Some felt they could never truly be integrated into American Society. Others feared their numbers and uprisings and determined they must be quelled by force. One faction held to the notion that a solution to the *problem* of freed slaves in America was to resettle them in a colony in Africa.

The American Colonization Society (ACS), whose members included politicians and religious leaders, brought this idea to fruition. Beginning in 1820, they sent ships from New York to West Africa filled with freed American slaves and agents of the ACS. This population of freed slaves was armed with both monetary and military support from the United States. They settled on the coast of what is now known as Liberia and established themselves as the ruling class. It would come to be that this very small population known as the America-Liberians would rule the entire region and maintain power until the civil wars of the twentieth century.

Eventually, support for ACS withered and their finances dried up during a time of European colonial expansion. "Faced with no source of revenue and an indecisive United States, the settlers declared their status as an independent country on 26 July 1847" (Lidow 145). They instituted a government modeled after the U.S., including a constitution and three branches of government. In fact, the first elected president of Liberia was a native of Norfolk, Virginia.

In the process of establishing their own customs and governance, they robbed the indigenous peoples of their freedoms. In response to Britain's and France's requirement that the Liberian Government secure its territory as a condition of sovereignty, the America-Liberians constructed a system of indirect rule—some would later call it jungle justice—where local chiefs acted as miniature heads of states. They collected taxes and laborers for public works projects. They were backed by a Liberian military force. "At least five large-scale revolts erupted in the first fifty years of independence and these were crushed with brutal force by the Liberian Frontier Force and other settler militias" (Levitt as cited by Lidow 146).

In 1931, the League of Nations reprimanded Liberia for its use of forced labor and slavery (Times of London as cited by Lidow 146). It was reported that this regime forcibly took young men and transported them to plantations where they would spend their days laboring under brutal conditions. Sound familiar? One has to pause and recoil at this, at man's propensity to sin: that a people would, upon gaining their freedom, inflict upon others the same cruelties they had endured themselves. Ed's own father, one of the indigenous peoples, was born into this cruel culture. Some called it forced labor. It was a brutal existence: mining rubber trees for latex, forests for timber and the ground for precious stones. Back-breaking work. There was no opportunity for education for either father or his children in rural Liberia where 95% of the population lived. There were no established schools. The villages were kept isolated and primitive.

Even more bizarre than the enslavement was the white southern culture the Americo-Liberians brought with them over the massive Atlantic waters. They erected quaint church buildings with steeples and wore top hats and white gloves to the services. There arose a new racism. Those with lighter skin, Anglo-American names and Anglo-American hair elevated themselves above the tribal peoples. The physical distinctions made this easy. For generations, Americo-Liberians held control of the government. The oppressive policies fostered a deep hatred among the tribal peoples for those in power.

The Americo-Liberians built schools and churches as part of a plan to *civilize* and *Christianize* the indigenous peoples. If one wants to eat the fruit of prosperity, one must become *civilized*: come to the city, to the city churches, to the city schools, be baptized, and learn to read. Consequently, if one had hopes of becoming educated, he or she had to leave the rural village and migrate to the capital, Monrovia, take up residence in a foster home and find a way to pay for schooling once enrolled. Ed's father felt, for the survival of the entire family, that one child should be sent to the city to be educated and thus could provide a better life for both the child and the entire family. Ed was chosen. He was only four years old.

Indeed, young Ed was sent to live with a relative in Monrovia with the intent to be nurtured and attend school. But this relative, a niece to Ed's father took this little boy and beat him forcing him to sell bread and other wares in the streets and then used the money he earned to send her own children to school. At the end of each day Ed would return with the money, she would count it, and if any was missing, she would beat him then, too. He watched his cousins go back and forth to the school he had been sent away from his own family to attend. *Four years old.* This was his way of life until he was 12.

Intermittently, he would run away but not to return to the village. It was so far away. Would he have remembered the way? Ed reports he became a child of the streets, participating in all their wayward activities. He found solace in the gangs of roving children that had been left to fend for themselves. The relative would find him, bring him home again and beat him. He would stay for a time, sell their wares, and then run again. Amazingly, word got back to his father that Ed was a street child, still uneducated, lost. It is hard to imagine the pain as such news sank into the ears and the hearts of Ed's mother and father. How agonizing it must have been to have parted with one of their own children, especially one so young, in hopes that such a move would benefit both the child and the family.

This desperate father set out on foot for Monrovia to find his beloved son, a three-week journey through snake-ridden, swollen creeks, thick unforgiving bush and very few roads. When he reached Monrovia, Ed was no longer with this family. The father took to the streets to find him, combing the alleyways looking for his son. Ed had left when he was only four years old, but now his father was looking for a young man of 12. How would he know him? But somehow, by the grace of God, he knew him right when he saw him. And he grabbed him and brought him to a place of lodging. They spent a night there before beginning their journey home, but in the middle of the night Ed slipped away and ran.

Ed shares that he had lost the desire for a father. So much time had passed without one. He felt he had been sold into slavery, and there was no child left in him. In his heart, there was no longer a place for a father. How many people, having endured unspeakable pain, or having given themselves over to sin, have lost their desire for our heavenly Father? In the Scriptures He calls to them, *Oh My people! Oh My people*! Oh my son! Oh my son! Imagine him awakening in the morning after the relief of having found him to see that he was gone, the room empty. Oh my child! Oh my son!

Ed's father took to the streets once again. But then, Ed knew he was looking for him. It would take his father three whole weeks of searching to recover his child again. This time he did not take the time to rest. He put his boy in an old grey pick-up truck loaded down with rusted barrels filled with latex from rubber trees. Bloody latex…the very treasure that men enslaved men for. They started for home.

2

In Perils of Waters

Here marks the beginning of Ed's journey home to his family, but more importantly, to the Lord.

The roads ended abruptly, and Ed and his father climbed down from the truck bed and journeyed on foot. He had no clothing other than what he wore. No shoes, no provisions. They had left in such haste. The rescue mission had already taken two long months. Away from the city, away from the city churches and away from the city streets, they encountered the bush. They faced miles and miles of thick brush. They waded through acres of swamps, venturing into cold, muddy water unable to see the snakes that were lurking. At times the water was up to Ed's chest, sometimes up to his neck. The creeks were so swollen, nearly swallowing them whole. The fast-moving waters ripped the clothes from his body stinging his eyes and nose as he went under and came up.

In cold and nakedness, he passed through waters with the scruff of his neck in the grip of his father's hand. In perils of waters his earthly father delivered his boy to a place where he would meet his heavenly Father. In dug-out canoes they crossed deep menacing creeks. Though his father knew how to swim, Ed could not. In perils of waters they made their way home to the place of his birth, but now as a young man.

There in the bush quite near his home village came an amazing turn of events. A missionary by the name of R.G. LeTourneau, a businessman from Texas, established a Christian school in Bafu Bay, practically in Ed's backyard. It was in Bafu Bay that Ed received an education. It was there in Bafu Bay that Ed received Christ.

This R.G. LeTourneau had brought the Gospel and reading and writing to the indigenous peoples of Liberia. God brought deliverance into the bush and freedom to these people.

As a teenager, Ed recalls towering over the five and six year old students in the beginning reading and mathematics classes. During all those years in Monrovia he had only learned survival on the streets. He was just now learning the fundamentals. The feelings of humiliation and disgrace still flood him today, he says, when he reflects on this time. But he did not allow them to control him. In fact, these feelings motivated him to study more diligently and to advance more quickly. He desperately wanted to be immersed in classrooms with students his own age and size. He studied day and night until he advanced to an age-appropriate level.

Ed could have quit very easily and run. Running was something he had done most of his life. But he is certain of this: God had His hand on him. He put a drive in him and gave him the maturity to understand that this would pass and that he would learn to read and write and that he would excel at mathematics. Not only did he persevere, but Ed also took the time to copy (by hand) all of the information from his textbooks and send it to his siblings at home. He wanted them to have the opportunity to learn as well. He became such a diligent student that he set his sights on attending medical school with dreams of delivering a healing ministry as a missionary doctor to his rural brothers and sisters.

Ed would return to Monrovia to attend high school, as there were no high schools near his village. Next he attended Tubman Institute for Medical Arts with an emphasis in nursing. After graduating and not yet having gone on to medical school, Ed yielded to a strong desire to return to his rural village. But the dream of becoming a missionary doctor never left him. He worked for a time at JFK Memorial Hospital as a nurse. He worked graveyard shifts, always nibbling the edges of practicing the kind of medicine of his dreams. Even to this day, if he allows himself, he can still feel the pang of desire to go to medical school and become a surgeon. I have seen the look of longing in his eyes as he would stand by my husband, a surgeon, while my husband operated on a Liberian patient, and suddenly I remember he is merely a man, made of flesh and blood and earthly desires.

After he graduated high school and returned to his county, Ed continued to grow in favor with men. He served in the local government as Municipal Commissioner. It was during this time that he made the most crucial decision of his life—second only to following Jesus Christ—and that was choosing a wife.

3

Cece

"It is not good for the man to be alone; I will make him a helper suitable for him...So the LORD God caused a deep sleep to fall upon the man, and he slept; then He took one of his ribs and closed up the flesh at that place. The LORD God fashioned into a woman the rib which He had taken from the man, and brought her to the man. The man said, 'This is now bone of my bones, and flesh of my flesh; She shall be called Woman because she was taken out of Man'" (Genesis 2:18-23).

And so the Lord looked upon Ed Kofi and fashioned a woman for him. Her name is Cecelia, or "Cece" as she prefers. A man like Ed would require no less than such a remarkable woman. She is a lioness: strong, yet elegant. Her light brown skin calls to mind the coming together of nations, her fullness of body calls to mind her gift as mother and protector, her soft melodic voice calls to mind secrets of sacrifice and service stored within her. He, with his commanding presence, quick but heavy gait and straight back and shoulders, still brings her before congregations to sing the sweet songs of his beloved Liberia. Standing next to her, just far enough away that she may have the microphone, he presents her and invites the congregation to experience his country through her song. She looks off into the distance, beyond us, as she sings. Her body shifts slowly from side to side, and the traditional sapphire blue headdress becomes a crown, her purple peasant dress a royal gown. We are transported to the bush, lush and green, barefoot, no longer in the church ministry center, swallowed by the wax green palm leaves, our eyes squinting from the cooking oil's smoke as the plantains fry. This choir of one allows Ed to keep the soul of Liberia with him always. His deep connection to her is evident in his expression as he watches her sing, his eyes now softened and fixed on hers. How the Lord has blessed them both with the gift of each other.

Theirs was an arranged marriage. Ed's mother loved Cece, and she wanted her as her own daughter. She went to Cece's mother and asked if she would allow her to be Ed's wife. Her mother said yes. But Cece, at first, upon seeing how much older Ed was, said no. Ed persisted, somehow knowing this quiet woman carried his future children within her and a steady faith to step outside of her vessel and walk onto waters.

Years later, but before their orphanage was even a thought in Ed's heart, he is certain that the willing heart of his wife to adopt his deceased brother's eight children prepared him for providing for Liberian orphans in their distress. Cece would give birth eight times and also mother her grieving nieces and nephews. They were building a marriage on the foundation of biblical commands: loving the Lord and loving others. The Kofi household would be a forerunner to the African Christian Fellowship International orphanage. Why would he stop with his brother's children? Why not also provide for his countrymen's?

"I will make a helper suitable for him." For Ed, it is Cece.

They enjoyed a quiet life in rural Liberia from 1975 to 1980. In 1980, Liberia started a long trek down a bloody path of coups and civil war.

4

In Perils of My Own Countrymen
(And the Beginning of ACFI)

Samuel Doe, a vicious (as described by Ed) military leader, brutally toppled the corrupt and oppressive Liberian government. By exploiting the hatred the indigenous peoples had for the Americo-Liberians, he successfully led a military coup as a master sergeant of the Liberian Army. Doe was of the Krahn tribe, a bushman of Grand Gedeh County. His newly deputized Head of State, Thomas Weh Syen, was of the Sarpo tribe. Ed, a bushman himself, was of the Kru tribe. The people of Sarpo and Kru tribes lived side-by-side in one county, and Doe's tribe lived in a neighboring county. All were from deep within the bush.

Doe did not simply oust the leaders and dissolve the powers of the Americo-Liberian governing body, but also systematically murdered supporters of William Tolbert, the sitting president. Ten days after he arose as leader of the new government, Doe publicly executed 13 of Tolbert's Cabinet members. He had them brought near the ocean, lined them up as though they were targets for practice, tied them to polls and shot them one by one in the open air. These were not soldiers, trained to face deadly weapons. These were bureaucrats, many in dress pants. Citizens and providers, unprepared and cut down, from the

Speaker of the House to the Chief Justice. Every day those seen as America-Liberians were arrested and, without trial or charges, executed.

Thomas Weh Syen, Doe's Deputy Head of State was uneducated and mentally unstable. He was overseeing various requests presented by different parties. If someone had a complaint or wished to gain permission to move from one government position to another, he was the go-to man. He ruled from his office. People streamed to his waiting room, a type of outer court, and waited for him to appear and direct them to speak. As though he were a judge of ancient Israel, he would hear complaints and make rulings. But instead of being filled with proverbial wisdom, he was mad. "A most vicious, cruel man," Ed says.

Ed traveled to Monrovia and made his way to this office to request permission to be released of his local government position. By this time, Ed had held several offices and was highly respected and well-liked among those at high levels. "That young man," those in leadership would say of Ed. "Bring him along with you," they would say to the mid-level leaders. As a result, the mid-level leaders were jealous. This particular position was a Municipal Commissioner, a highly-respected position. The upheaval provided an opportunity for ambitious men to have Ed eliminated. A group of accusers including some of Ed's own Kru tribe gathered together and elected a spokesman. They filed in and lined the walls of Weh Syen's outer court, arriving just before Ed.

Ed took a seat in a vacant spot on a long couch. The room

was crowded; bodies milling around, some entering and exiting, nervously slamming doors. An insane man uttered nonsense to no one, adding to the confusion. Outside, people scrambled as the reality of the violent coup took hold. That very day, when Ed was at the State Capital building, arrests were being made. The Minister for Local Government had urged Ed to go to Weh Seyn and ask to be relieved of his position. And so here he was, sitting still, nervously waiting to see this ruthless new leader.

Weh Syen appeared. He surveyed the room and addressed the men lining the wall opposite Ed.

"Why are you here?" he blurted at them.

"We are here," the spokesman stated, "to make a complaint against THAT man." He pointing directly at Ed.

Ed started.

"He is evil, a killer, a ruthless man!" the spokesman accused. Nods and a chorus of slurs of agreements came from the others.

Fear paralyzed Ed and made him mute. *What was he doing there? Why was he there?* His mind was slow to reset.

Weh Syen bounded over to Ed, sat on the coffee table, eyes glaring, no more than a foot away and asked, "What do you have to say?"

Ed sat defenseless.

"What do you have to say?" Weh Syen barked.

No answer.

But, as abruptly as he had barked at Ed, Weh Syen turned away and spoke to the insane man leaning against a wall adjacent to the accusers.

"What do *you* have to say about this case?" the mad man

spoke to the mad man.

Slowly, lucidly, miraculously, the insane man spoke. "These people should not have come to you," he motioned toward the plaintiffs. "They should have taken their case to court."

Weh Syen turned to Ed's accusers. "Each of you," he roared, "out of my office now, or else I will have you executed!"

The men hurried out of the room, but tried to gain footing with yet a different high ranking official who was present in the hallway. This man too, the Deputy Speaker, commanded them to leave, uttering similar threats. At the same moment, Weh Syen was releasing Ed from government work.

Within one year's time, Weh Syen himself would be executed, suspected of plotting to overthrow Doe. And so it went during the long and bloody era of betrayals and perils amongst their own countrymen.

Now hear Ed's heart: the man who served as the spokesman against Ed, the one who voiced the accusations that very easily could have culminated in Ed's death, came to know and follow Ed and become one of his interpreters. Ed freely forgave him. *Freely you have received, and so freely give,* Ed's Master commands in Matthew 10:8. The man became a loyal defender because he saw the miracle of God, Ed says. In this man, Ed sees God's unfailing grace.

When Ed was a young man, he thought he could use the government to help his people. He thought the government positions were going to give him the power to serve his own countrymen. But here we see two things: his very own countrymen yearned for and plotted his death, and his country's government became more interested in sustaining itself than serving its people.

"But God," Ed says, "used an insane man as my defender, my lawyer, my rescuer." Soon after these events, Doe offered Ed a position in his government. He wanted to appoint him as Development Superintendent. On his journey to Doe's home county, Ed stopped along the way to visit his own mother. She asked him why he was visiting the Head of State's hometown. Ed told her of Doe's intentions. She wisely guided him, saying, "No. God intervened in your life not so that you would serve the government." She gathered prayer at a one week long mission conference that Ed would restrain himself from taking any position. Ed is convinced that prayer changes things. He has never served in the government since.

Ed is clear that faith alone in God is key. Sadly, his loyal interpreter did not come to that place of understanding. At first, during his years as Ed's interpreter, Ed described him as most loyal and grew to love him. When people would bring up "the old piece," as Ed puts it, how he had sought to have Ed killed, Ed was grieved to be reminded. He felt it was so wrong. He would say that this was a man whom God had changed. During their time spent side-by-side Ed grew close to this man's family. Yet, despite his close connection to Ed, years later, he unfortunately got caught up in what many called "Freedom Fighting" under Charles Taylor. Ed was out of the country at that time. Those who coined this term did not understand that Charles Taylor had an agenda based on revenge, greed and power, hardly the makings of freedom. The interpreter, like so many others, had misguided fervor, misplaced trust. After the interpreter's death, a death on the battlefield serving as one of Charles Taylor's generals, Ed became as a father to the man's son. He died, Ed says, because he did not remain faithful to God alone.

Do you not know? Have you not heard? Has it not been declared to you from the beginning? Have you not understood from the foundations of the earth? It is He who sits above the circle of the earth and its inhabitants are like grasshoppers Who stretches out the heavens like a curtain And spreads them out like a tent to dwell in; He it is who reduces rulers to nothing, Who makes the judges of the earth meaningless. Scarcely have they been planted, scarcely have they been sewn, scarcely has their stock taken root, But He merely blows on them, and they wither, and the storm carries them away like stubble.

"To whom then will you liken me that I would be his equal?" says the Holy One. Lift up your eyes on high and see who created these stars, the One who leads forth their host by number; He calls them all by name. Because of the greatness of His might and the strength of His power, not one of them is missing.
(Isaiah 40: 21-26)

The Beginning of ACFI

Ed was now free, by God's provision, from serving in the government. Once free he brought Cece to Monrovia. Once free, he could devote all his time to Christ's Church.

Several years earlier Ed had become acquainted with Bishop Marwieh of the Association of Independent Churches of Africa (AICA). Bishop Marwieh mentored Ed, and Ed grew in faith and gained invaluable knowledge of missionary work. He became a full-time Pastor of AICA and participated in spreading the Gospel through this church from 1981-1986. He was so zealous for the church's work that Marwieh appointed him to the position of Executive Secretary. As he served, he felt a desire to reach the most isolated regions of Liberia and across country borders. He was developing his own vision and direction for the church.

In his personal life, he was living out the commands of his Master, Jesus Christ, given in the Sermon on the Mount. Despite the cruel treatment he had endured at the hands of his father's niece in Monrovia when he was a small boy, Ed honored her in death by giving her a proper burial. He tended to her without a thread of bitterness. Before her death, she spoke highly of him, saying to others how proud she was of him and what an honorable young man he grew to be.

There came a time when Ed would leave the headship of Bishop Marwieh and no longer serve under the umbrella of AICA. Bishop Marwieh recognized Ed's gifts: his strong leadership skills, his zeal for the Gospel, his intellect, and his ease in relating to all kinds of people. So when Ed approached Marwieh, asking for his blessing to start an independent, indigenous, evangelical church, Bishop Marwieh let him go.

His vision was to go from village to village reaching the

untouched parts of Liberia. Yet while in Monrovia, Ed could not look past the extreme poverty and hopelessness that filled the slums of the capital. He saw a great void, and knew that only the Word of God and the Gospel of Jesus Christ could fill it. The Scripture, "Follow Me, and I will make you fishers of men" (Mark 1:17) comes to mind as Ed saw the people's desperation for basic medical care. He saw it as an opportunity. "We would get them in the door," he said, "by offering simple medical treatment: cleaning and bandaging open wounds, treating dehydration and diarrhea. But then we would offer them words of eternal life." This place was known as the Buzzi Quarters clinic. Still today, this clinic exists to serve the needs of the poor.

It was here that African Christian Fellowship International (ACFI) was born; here in the shadows cast by the presidential palace in the poorest slum of Monrovia, a stone's throw from the high walls that guarded the Head of State's windows and doors. Ed birthed a ministry in the midst of people living on top of people without running water. Through this poorest of districts ran an open sewer, which, under flooding conditions, filled the streets with human excrement. It is no surprise that our God, who delivered His own Son in the humblest of settings, blessed this ministry. This clinic, this Buzzi Quarters urban clinic, was only the beginning.

ACFI flourished. The clinic was a launching pad. Ed expanded from this healing and evangelizing ministry to also training young men to take the Gospel to the interior. They were sent out and went from village to village and county to county. They planted churches and established schools. Many

Liberians became citizens of the Kingdom of God who had lived their whole lives practicing ancestor worship, witchcraft and animism; people previously blind to the truth and light. The Word was going out across the land changing hearts, but all the while the wounds of the tribal rivalries festered. Another violent wave was coming like labor pains increasing in strength, relentless and advancing.

Charles Taylor, a begrudged former participant in the Doe government who had been ousted for embezzlement was stoking deep animosities in neighboring Ivory Coast, a haven for Liberians who had fled from Nimba County when Doe had slaughtered civilians following an uprising under Thomas Quiwonkpa. Doe had not only slaughtered those behind the attempted coup, but also slaughtered their fellow tribal people, those of the Gio and Mano tribes (Lidow 150). While ACFI was preparing the Liberian people for the coming of Jesus Christ, Charles Taylor was preparing a rebellion that would prove far bloodier than anything the Liberian people could have imagined.

5

In Journeys Often

"On Christmas Eve 1989, about a hundred rebels crossed into Liberia from Cote d'Ivoire (Ivory Coast) and captured the border town of Butuo, Nimba County...Taylor formed the group by recruiting former AFL (national military) soldiers, mostly ethnic Gio and Mano, who fled Doe's purges in 1984-1985 and settled in refugee camps in Cote d'Ivoire. Within days of the invasion, Taylor announced on BBC World Service the arrival of the National Patriotic Front of Liberia (NPFL). The NPFL quickly gained momentum...town after town fell to the NPFL as Doe's soldiers withdrew from hostile territory" (Lidow 151).

In February of 1990, four years into ACFI's work, Ed and Cece journeyed to the United States to plead for help from the American churches. They were certain that they had ample time as the rebellion was in the interior. Their hope was that churches would send support in the form of monetary aid and relief supplies since the civil war, which was ravaging parts of the interior, had taken its toll on ACFI's ability to minister. The poor became destitute. The Deaf and blind were in need of protection while food was becoming scarcer, inflating the price of rice, the staple of the Liberian diet. It was becoming increasingly difficult to provide for all the needs laid at the feet of ACFI. Let the reader understand the perception of America that most Liberians have. They see America as being a perfect place, as told by numerous Liberians, where there is an abundance and collective willingness to save and provide for the afflicted. It has been said that in the midst of the carnage, had there been only a modest showing of American troops, the mere sight of their uniforms and flag would have caused most to lay down their weapons. It made sense for Ed and Cece to journey to America, appear before churches and ask for assistance. They left their children in Monrovia, certain the rebels would not make it near the capital.

What happened next, happened quickly. Charles Taylor's NPFL descended upon Monrovia, as did a splinter faction under Prince Yormie Johnson. Johnson had led the Taylor invasion in Nimba but became frustrated with Taylor's inability to deliver on certain promises, so he formed another rebel faction: the Independent National Patriotic Front of Liberia (INPFL). Johnson's troops captured the western suburbs of Monrovia, while Taylor's troops controlled the north (Lidow 151-153). Doe was holed up in his presidential palace. Ed and Cece watched the horror unfold on a television from their room in the United States. At the same time, a bounty had been put on Ed's head. A group of pastors had formed a peace march and taken to the streets of Monrovia, asking Doe to step down to put an end to the violence and allow an international interim government to step in. Doe responded by having the pastors beaten and thrown in prison. Taylor would also issue orders to have Ed executed. Ed would find himself caught in crisis after crisis involving death warrants, seen as a potential threat to each warlord's swipe for absolute power. Returning to Liberia meant certain death for Ed at this time.

Ed and Cece decided that Cece would return to protect the children and Ed would follow. Expecting that the United States would intervene, the couple felt they needed to simply provide for their children and wait hopefully. They were wrong. The United States never intervened.

Months passed. Cece and the children languished inside the besieged city, and it was no longer possible for Ed to journey in. The borders were closed. Ed moved in and out of his days in the U.S. as if dead. Had he sent his wife and the mother of his children to a certain death? In his mind he replayed the decision over and over again. *You go. This will die down soon. I will come when they come to understand I am no threat and lift the bounty on my head. Nobody will stop you from reaching the children.*

Despair set in. A fellow missionary encouraged him to go to Sierra Leone. *Go to Sierra Leone,* he said. *Fly there. At least you will be closer to your countrymen, closer to your wife and children.* Many Liberian refugees were in Sierra Leone. *Perhaps,* the friend counseled, *you can learn of Cece and the children's welfare and whereabouts from another Liberian. Perhaps, from such a close distance, you can get to them by land.* So Ed journeyed to Sierra Leone.

6

In Perils of Robbers

Freetown. Freetown, Sierra Leone. Liberian refugees rushed there like water rushing down a drain, hundreds of thousands having fled the bush. Machete-wielding rebels, blinded by their desire to take vengeance on Americo-Liberians, ravaged and maimed their countrymen on their rampage toward Monrovia. Fleeing mothers drowned their precious crying infants in rivers to silence their cries in the hopes of saving the many others crouching in the waters. Fleeing in terror. Rebel-teenaged boys, delirious with drugs and rage, cruelly decapitated elder men in front of their wives and children. Decapitated, castrated, raped, tortured. Fleeing in terror. Snakes, malaria. Fleeing, fleeing into Sierra Leone and other bordering countries. Mobs of the terrorized, terror-stricken, hunted and seemingly forsaken rushed into Sierra Leone, Guinea and Ivory Coast.

In an effort to get closer to Cece and the children who were still in exile and unable to reenter Liberia, Ed had made his way from the United States and was then among some of these refugees in Sierra Leone. These weary, battered souls had found their way over the border of their homeland and into a country where they would be collectively despised. They were like lepers. The scourge of society, blamed for crimes and crowding, and eventually for Sierra Leone's own civil war they were seen as leeches and troublemakers. No one wanted them there. But there they were in a place called Freetown.

The United Nations was present and working to provide food for the refugees while more and more people arrived. Ed sought lodging and stayed at a motel for a time. When Ed was away from his rented room, thieves entered and stole most of his money. There was no evidence of forced entry, no marks on the door and no broken windows. It was obvious to Ed that this had been an inside job. The police were summoned to investigate at the manager's request. They reasoned that a key was used to gain entry. Ed explains that the workers, in all likelihood, knew that he was a Liberian refugee, and, as some Sierra Leone people had no regard for Liberians, they felt they could do anything to him. Some felt a refugee should not be given the same rights and protections under the Sierra Leone law. So they robbed him. But the police investigated. They followed through as best they could. The money was not recovered, but they took the motel workers to the police station for questioning. The owner became infuriated. Being a woman of great influence within this community, she expelled Ed and then proceeded to blackball him from other motels.

Ed knocked on one door after another asking for vacancies, but no one would take him in. This experience had to feel strange, as he had enjoyed years of great favor. It seemed whatever he touched had thrived under the good hand of God, first in the government work and then with the ministry in Buzzi Quarters and the flowering of ACFI. And yet how he must have also had the all-too familiar twinge of his childhood pains: unwanted, on the streets, looking into vacant faces, his hands in his empty pockets.

He wandered into an old abandoned frame house. He was barely standing and exhausted in mind and body. He entered through the fractured door and lay on the crude floor. Surrounded by remnants of walls, he looked up at the ceiling. The trusses hung over him, strung together like ribs. The gnawing pain of extreme hunger gripped his insides. But it was the deep ache that he felt for his Cece, the agony of thinking her dead that strained him so. How the decision for her to return haunted him! And what of his children? He looked up at the trusses and considered his helplessness.

He closed his eyes and wept. One man, one faithful man lay in seeming defeat.

For You had cast me into the deep, into the heart of the seas, and the current surrounded me. All Your breakers and billows passed over me. So I said, "I have been expelled from Your sight."
(Jonah 2:3-4a)

Ed slept in the belly of this old abandoned frame house for two days.

When he finally emerged, he happened upon a Christian acquaintance who had family in Sierra Leone. He thanked God and followed the man to his parents' house. The young man's father was blind and a devout Muslim, married to a woman who had Christian sons. He knew Ed was a Christian preacher and, by the grace of God, still took him in. Consider God's sovereignty here. Not only did he care for Ed, but Ed would use this home as a base as he launched an ACFI church in Sierra Leone. The son became Ed's first disciple in Sierra Leone. Many people would come to the home to ask for Pastor Kofi to pray for them. This father allowed such activities when, in the past, he had shown himself to be unfriendly and even hostile to outsiders.

A passage comes to mind from the Book of Isaiah, when the Lord prophesies through Isaiah, more than 100 years before King Cyrus is born, that He will use Cyrus one day as His servant. History reveals that this King Cyrus would be the one in Persia who would issue a decree to let the captive Israelites return to Jerusalem to rebuild the temple. King Cyrus himself did not know the Lord. "It is I who says of Cyrus, he is My shepherd! He will perform all I desire. And he declares of Jerusalem, 'she will be built,' and of the temple, 'your foundation will be laid'...I have also called you by your name; I have given you a title of honor though you have not known Me" (Isaiah 44:28, 45:4b). Ed was honored in this family as they gave him a room for lodging they had used for their very own children.

Ed regained his strength. He knew he was helpless to find his wife and children at this time, but was consumed by the agony of not protecting his dear bride or his children. He kept watch for Liberian refugees in public places in hopes that he could inquire about his family. There were some from ACFI who had made it to Sierra Leone and the news they carried was always dire. They and others gathered under Ed's leadership for prayer meetings and encouragement. This was a time of waiting, praying and keeping watch with other refugees.

On New Year's Day, Ed was resting when he became aware of the Lord pressing upon him to reach the masses of refugees with the Gospel. Daily, Ed saw both fear and emptiness in their eyes as he moved among the people, a look unique to the war-torn and wandering. In his heart he knew his priority was finding a way to get to Cece. But a voice inside of him was clear, the Holy Spirit redirecting him away from his personal desires. He felt the Lord questioning him, "What does it mean to 'cast your burdens upon the Lord?' Once you have given Me your cares in prayer, I am in charge." He explains in his Liberian accent, "You don't handle something that you've already turned over to Jesus. I entrusted my family to His care. It is a very difficult thing to do to accept that I am powerless to rescue my own wife. What was left for me to do was right in front of me." He resolved, in obedience, to go and reach the Liberians who were there.

Ed searched for a place in a central location to start an outreach program. He gathered together men of faith who were Sierra Leone nationals, and they came to a large home with three bedrooms and a spacious plaza. The location was ideal. With the help of his Christian brothers, he leased the property and began having meetings and Bible studies there. Ed involved some local evangelists and a youth pastor. He also made an appeal to friends in the United States. Remember the journey to the States to garner support for ACFI in the early phase of the war? These same connections bore fruit in Sierra Leone. The

Lord provided through these American churches abundantly. Massive containers arrived from across the Atlantic Ocean filled with relief supplies: nonperishable foods, Bibles, clothing, shoes, to name a few. This center house became a renowned haven to the refugees. They came to be fed and clothed. They came and heard the Gospel of Jesus Christ and countless souls were added to the Kingdom of heaven. Ed, to this day, marvels at the abundant supply provided by the grace of God. They launched a lunchtime ministry and every day a meal was provided along with the Word of God. This ministry soared.

War came to Sierra Leone and raged from 1991-2001. A brutal rebel group, the Revolutionary United Front (RUF), descended upon the Liberian refugee camps, kidnapping and proselytizing the most vulnerable and the orphaned in their attempts to overthrow the Sierra Leone government. Liberian warlord Charles Taylor, the architect of child soldier warfare, supported the RUF by trading with them diamonds for guns and allowing them to use Liberia as a supply route. At the height of the RUF activity, revenue from illicit diamond sales brought in $125 million annually (Global Witness 2012).

Liberian refugees became enemies of the state and were seen as consorting with the rebels. The United Nations distribution centers became snares. Security forces would station themselves there, watch for Liberian refugees seeking relief, and then arrest them. It did not take long for the refugees to know it was deadly to get aid from the U.N. But God had a plan. He had already set His servant, Ed, in a position to provide. Word traveled that Ed's lunchtime ministry was a safe haven. Ed never had to turn away anyone. The containers kept coming and Ed emerged as a trustworthy person. Those Sierra Leone countrymen who now suffered amidst their own civil war also came to the center to be fed. The alien became the shepherd. God's ways are most certainly not our ways. As this ministry went on, so did church planting throughout much of the country beyond Freetown. Pastors were raised up, equipped and sent out to uphold Christ's Church throughout the land. Ed reports that the ACFI church that stands in Sierra Leone today, under national leadership, was born out of this lunchtime ministry.

Ed was physically present to launch this church, in country. But that meant that he had been separated from his family, on and off, for four years. This is a long time to be away during peace time, but war! He had not been despondent, but instead had been diligent. Although he would come to know of his family's whereabouts during this time period, he also knew they could perish in the Liberian war on any given day. Yet, he was at work, like a Zerubbabel building the temple of the Living God, or a Nehemiah rebuilding the wall that guarded Jerusalem. These great men had enormous burdens set upon their shoulders amidst tremendous opposition. They did not pass off the burden to another in order to tend to their own concerns. They knew their God, and they did not shrink back. They are witnesses to the power of our great and awesome God; men such as these.

Nevertheless I will look again toward Your holy temple...
While I was fainting away, I remembered the LORD,

and my prayer came to You, Into Your holy temple...
That which I have vowed I will pay. Salvation is from the LORD.
(Jonah 2:4b, 7, 9b)

Part II

7

The Cost

I will not leave you as orphans
(John 14:18a)

What would one pay to buy the freedom of a people? Would he or she pay with the currency of the life of a child? No parent would say yes, knowingly. And yet, that is what our heavenly Father did. He bought our freedom with the life of His Beloved Son.

All wars have casualties. It is inevitable. While Ed was in exile in Sierra Leone, Cece and the children languished in Monrovia. They began to starve. The streets were filled with roving teen-aged boys, guns strapped to their backs and eyes hard as stone, poised to take whatever they wanted: a bag of rice, a pot of water, a child. Finding food became a necessary but deadly mission.

On this particular day, with Cece so weak, four of her daughters set out. It was far more dangerous for the males to venture out. The males were either kidnapped or summarily eliminated by warring factions or by suspicious civilians. Guns, bombs and machetes, unlike food, were in abundance.

There, in the midst of the chaos, stood an open market by the St. Paul Bridge. Such an open market would seem to be a trap, a place to lure people out of hiding, out into the open. But yet people would surface to exchange goods for food, money for food. Sitting here, in America, it seems obvious to us that the children should not go there, where even the rebels and the corrupt government soldiers participated. But most Americans have no experience with starvation. Most do not know how it feels to stand with their skeletal frames like wire hangers and their skin like drapery with little in between. The girls went to the bridge, desperate. Four went out. One was taken. Only three returned.

So began a season of captivity for Ed and Cece's oldest daughter, Lucy. Seventeen months in the hands of the rebels. That is five hundred nights and five hundred days. Cece would hear the news of her daughter's capture, and so began her season of a thousand rains.

At the tender age of 13, Lucy's reality became as that of an orphan: the ground beneath her became hard, and the roads before her and behind her disappeared.

So great a price our Savior paid: His precious blood spattered up and down the road to Calvary. Our salvation cost Him everything and us nothing. And here we stand on this side of the cross wanting all to know of His great love and mercy. Our Father knows of the pain of watching His Son suffer. He allowed it so that we might have life abundant.

Although Ed and Cece would one day see Lucy again—she would not be left in captivity, but rescued—what they say of their daughter today is that her mind is gone. She is no longer there. But even that is only for a time.

8

Lucy's Rescuer

I will come to you
(John 14:8b)

There is a Liberian man named Wleh Peters, or Thomas Peters in English, whom Ed describes as his most beloved disciple and a courageous young man. Thomas was of the Kru tribe, the same tribe as Ed, and from the same county. They did not meet in childhood, though. Thomas would not come to know Ed until Thomas was a young man.

There is a saying that behind every great man there is a great woman, and so this saying applies to both of these men as well. But often at the right hand of every great man there is another great man, one that propels the other forward in his mission and tends to matters closest to the leader's heart, thereby freeing him to lead. This right-hand man, content to be a warhorse for ACFI's missions and for Ed personally, is Thomas Peters. According to Thomas, if the head of a mission is cut off the whole body dies. He would risk his life over and over again in the midst of the civil war to minister to Ed and to provide for Ed's wife and children while Ed was in exile and planting churches in Sierra Leone and Nigeria. Ed has often emphasized that there were many faithful, courageous people whom God provided to love and protect his children during his absences. Ed's own sister Susie, whom Ed describes as a loving woman much like their mother, cared for his children time and time again. She among other humble and willing servants served as protector and surrogate mother and father in perilous times. God provided many hands and hearts. This book cannot contain all of their stories, and so these have been selected as they are the ones most familiar to our congregation here at Fellowship Bible Church of Tacoma.

As for Thomas Peters' involvement, one of the rescue missions he embarked upon was the rescue of Ed and Cece's oldest daughter from the hands of the rebels.

I ask the reader to consider these remarks as further evidence of God's abundant supply of grace and mercy. Many names of humble servants may not be written on these pages.

Let the reader also consider this opportunity to stop and admire God's heart and ways, so abundantly higher and more complex than man's. Man would choose, as a hero of a story, someone well-credentialed and respectable according to the world's standards, someone highly educated with a name well-recognized, with family connections and a physical stature to match. In the Old Testament it is written that Saul towered over his peers which won him favor, a king for the people. David, a mere shepherd boy who was considered the runt of his brothers would have gone unnoticed had God left the decision up to man. The Scriptures reveal that God sees not as man sees, as man looks at the outward appearance, but God looks at the heart (1Sam 16:7). Oskar Schindler was a man whom most modern-day church members would not have chosen to be a hero. He was an ethnic German who, during the rise of Nazi Germany, was a womanizer and partier. He was a businessman who entered into a hero's arena by buying factories and employing Jews. He would be used by God to save over 1000 Jews during the Holocaust. That population of over 1000 swelled to over 8000 in recent years. He died in Germany penniless (Bulow). An unlikely hero.

Thomas Peters was the only son of his mother and had six sisters. His father had twenty children by many different wives from Liberia and became a highly respected, high ranking police officer in Sierra Leone. But Thomas never knew him. There was no father in his life, other than God, until he came to know Ed. His family was very poor. Thomas and his half-brother (while in fifth and sixth grade) supported the family by collecting and selling empty glass bottles.

Thomas met Ed when Ed was a pastor for AICA under Bishop Marwieh. When the conferences came to his area, AICA members provided luncheons and church services. Thomas would go for the food but not continue on in the church. "When the food was gone, I was gone," he says. He also shares that he was baptized three times in his life. The first was in an Episcopal church as a small boy. It meant nothing to him. The second baptism happened when a "prophet" came to town. He was baptizing people in the river. Thomas and some friends had been playing soccer in the hot sun. They were eager to go for a swim and cool off. When they approached the river, they saw a long line of people formed from well beyond the banks and extended on into the river where the "prophet" was waist high in water immersing people. Thomas' friends went home, but Thomas took a place in line. When it was his turn, he was immersed and, instead of coming up and into the man's hands, he stayed in the water and swam away, delighted to be cool and wet.

When he was a young man he was recruited into an organization as a paid informant. It was during his time infiltrating bars to gather information that he became an alcoholic. "I drank first thing in the morning and the last thing at night," Thomas says. His pay was twenty dollars per week, what others made in a month. He squandered his money on riotous living—booze, women—and had no plans for his future. "The alcohol will kill you," his mother warned him again and again. But this talk, Thomas laments, meant nothing to him. It disappeared into the spinning room as he lay on his bed with his eyes closed.

One of his sisters was pregnant and in labor and was admitted to the hospital. She endured a Cesarean Section and lost a tremendous amount of blood. All the nearest relatives were urgently summoned to the hospital. Each was tested to see if he or she qualified to donate blood for her. None qualified, except for Thomas. But when the providers saw the amount of alcohol in his blood, they refused to let him give. His mother looked at him and said *if your sister dies it will be your fault.* Thomas fled to another part of the hospital and wept bitterly. That night, he put away the alcohol. Months later the Lord would get a hold of a sober Thomas' heart through a song he had heard many times but had meant nothing to him. On this night as the lyrics sank in he gave his life to the Lord.

It's me again, Lord, I have a prayer. I need an answer.
It's me again, Lord, I have a problem I cannot solve...
Lord, I know you are busy in heaven...
But you promised that if I ask I will receive, so I am asking,
begging on my knees.

Thomas set his heart to become a disciple of Jesus Christ. Ed Kofi became his pastor, mentor and friend. And for the third time, Thomas was baptized. But this time it meant something.

When it came time for Ed to branch out from AICA and to become the head of a new church (ACFI), Thomas and others followed him. Thomas smiles as he tells of ACFI's first church meeting. They met in the upper floor of a Seaman's club. Sailors, after being out at sea for months, would come to these clubs searching for women and alcohol. The first floor of this building was filled with carousing and drunkenness. In the upper room the Word was being spoken and heard, praises and hymns were being sung and prayers were being uttered. Ed encouraged the small group that good things come from such places. God's ways are not our ways.

They moved to the Buzzi Quarters clinic and started worshiping there after a time. ACFI was taking root. Thomas was educated at one of the AICA schools. He attended with Ed's brother-in-law, Randolph. They graduated and received their first assignment to go out into the mission field. At that time,

Thomas found a wife as an answer to prayer.

God would deliver a gift to him by the name of Tukutu (pronounce too-koo-too with no syllable accented over the others). A sweet, simple name carried by a steady woman. Uncomplicated and meek, she is a God-fearing wife, Thomas says. And just as God will often reveal a hero from within an unlikely exterior, He also can disguise the heart of a lion inside a timid coat. This Tukutu, during one of the surges of the war, would be left alone, eight months pregnant, and concerned that the baby was no longer moving. Thomas was out on a food-finding mission and would not return. This Tukutu, then told that her husband was dead, would give birth to her still-born child and find the strength to survive. This Tukutu currently lives in Pennsylvania in a tiny home with seventeen Liberians, some of whom she took in during the wars, never to be separated even all these years later. Thomas says that during the inception of ACFI and also during the perils of the war, he would not be able to spend more than four days at a time with his wife and children. Underneath the timid exterior, this wife Thomas chose is a rock.

Thomas' first assignment was in Grand Gedeh County, while his partner, Randolph, was assigned to Nimba County. Along the way, they stopped and spent time with a family in Grand Gedeh County. These were farming villages. The whole family labored in the fields until nightfall. Dinner was served at nine o'clock. Randolph wandered into a local market and saw a snake cut into pieces and set out as meat for purchase. "They have long man in the market," he told Thomas, eyes open wide, upon his return. The two marveled that their countrymen ate snake. That night their host family rejoined them after coming in from the fields. Darkness had already set in and the family and their guests gathered around the fire for dinner. The men were enjoying their greens when Thomas' mouthful melted into bones. He felt them between his fingers but couldn't identify them in the dark. Randolph commented, "This looks like long man." The woman replied, "Oh yes, this is good meat for you. Boa Constrictor." Thomas' and Randolph's mouths stopped moving. "We had no choice but to keep eating. We were here to start a church, and God says all things are good to eat. We did not want to offend." So they held their breath and ate. Thomas still, all these years later, has pursed lips as he shares this story.

The two men continued on until they reached their assignments. Thomas' time in Toetown, Grand Gedeh County was not without difficulties. While he was busy starting an ACFI elementary school and pastoring a church, his place of lodging was burglarized. Thomas had given a leather bag to a woman who was keeping clothing in it. The bag and its contents were stolen, and the woman reported the items missing. Thomas describes something he refers to as *jungle justice*. In such remote areas there is corruption in law enforcement where a crime is exploited and used to extract money from anyone associated with an event, even just by proximity. Thomas knew this was a problem and wanted to protect the elderly people who lived in the home where the crime was committed. He had them leave the premises for a time so that they would not be taken to the local jail and then have to pay a bribe to be released. After the home was cleared, Thomas was then accused of the theft. "Why would I steal my own bag?" he asked them. But his protests were rebuffed. He was hauled off to jail.

When the ACFI missionary came to Toetown to check on Thomas, he asked, "Where is our pastor?"

"He is in jail," the people answered, pointing in the direction of the cinder-blocked shanty.

Thomas was released into the hands of the visiting missionary.

The school Thomas had started began to grow. Teaching children from a biblical worldview was completely new to these people. The competing schools were still participating in events contrary to the teachings of the Bible. Many transferred their children to the ACFI school. This created animosity between the leaders of the old school and the new. On Independence Day there was a parade. The kids attending the Christian school abstained from participating in the parade. "Some of the dances were designed to worship the devil, so we did not want our children participating," Thomas explains. This outraged many of the leaders and, for a second time in his short missionary life, he was put in jail.

The earnings of an ACFI missionary were twenty dollars per term (a four-month period). He would send the money to Tukutu to buy milk for the baby. She did have the support of her mother. Thomas was grateful. He loved the work. "This was grassroots stuff," he says, "I never minded the poor pay. We were taking part in the building of a church and taking it across the country. God provided," he says with peace in his eyes.

Imagine his thrill as a young man. After experiencing a life of severe poverty and then acquiring wealth tied to corruption, he now had the opportunity to live honorably; a life he never knew was possible until Ed took him under his wing. The Lord says, "I give you peace, not as the world gives..."

Imagine, also, what this activity looked like in the spiritual realm: people with strongholds held captive to sin and death being penetrated with the Gospel, freedom and eternal life! The enemy of our Lord and of His people would not leave this work alone without attempting to grab it by the throat and choke the life out of it.

"Did Ed tell you about the accident?" Thomas asks as we sit across the dining room table from one another after midnight. "No," I answered as I entered his last sentence. Then I caught his expression and stopped. His countenance changed dramatically, his eyes and head dropped. Then his shoulders rose as he took in a deep breath.

"ACFI held a conference in a nearby city in our county. I took people from Toetown to attend. Things had been going so well for ACFI. We all felt like we were a part of something good. At this conference small things went bad. A generator burned up and there was a disturbance caused by a military man as his aggressive advances toward a young woman were rebuffed. People had control over it though. But on the way back from the conference Ed waved our car to stop and said we should go back to base, to Monrovia, to retrieve some things and then return." Thomas got out of his car and joined the small caravan heading back to Monrovia. The two vans were overloaded with passengers. There was confusion in regards to one of the drivers. He went only as far as a certain city, and then he insisted that he would not go on. The group chartered another van.

It was late and very dark as the two vans neared a checkpoint. Unknown to them, a massive truck hauling long planks of timber was stopped at the checkpoint at the bottom of a hill. For some reason, perhaps because of the length of time that the government soldiers had held him at the checkpoint, the driver had turned off all of the vehicle's lights.

Thomas was in the lead van and Ed was in the van behind his. As they approached the checkpoint, they were gathering momentum down the hill. An oncoming truck had on its high beams. The bright light blinded the drivers, and then suddenly, a jolt and a noise—thud—deep and heavy, piercing, crashing. And then another. Thomas' van had careened into the back of the heavy-laden truck, and then Ed's van had crashed into Thomas's.

What happened next, Thomas cannot explain in any other way than to credit God's hand. When Thomas came to himself he was standing in the road unharmed. He extended his arms out and shook his head back and forth, still stunned. Weeping and wailing poured out of the second vehicle. Approaching his crumpled van smashed against the timber truck, he attempted to pull the nearest passenger out of the wreckage. "My hands couldn't grip her arm. I kept trying to pull her by her arm, but it was so soaked with blood. My grip kept slipping off." When another vehicle approached from the other direction, its headlights shone on the passengers, and Thomas saw, in a flash, that the woman on whose arm he was pulling had no head.

Thomas jumped back in confusion and scanned the scene. The driver also was decapitated. There were many who perished in that awful accident. *Many.* Thomas was amazed that he was spared and thanked Jesus. He and a two month old baby were the only two to survive completely unharmed. Both were miraculously outside the van.

At the hospital, Ed found Thomas and asked him if he was okay. Thomas assured him he was, and Ed told him to make a list of those critical and those dead and then take the news to town.

"I searched the hospital and was also taken to the morgue. It was filled with bodies. One man lost his sight. Some came to the States for treatment. The wakes and funerals were not easy. All the funeral cars in the city were needed. It was something that no one will ever forget."

One has to wonder what most people would have done after such a tremendous loss under such violent circumstances in regards to launching a ministry. Would many have perceived it as a sign that this church should not continue to spread and grow, questioning all that had been done so far and then aborting?

Our pastor has a saying when addressing some people's notions regarding faith: "That sounds spiritual, but it's not biblical." The history of the "tribe" of Christians (as the first century Romano-Jewish historian, Josephus, referred to the first followers of Jesus Christ) is full of tragedy and triumph. Many were martyred for not recanting their faith, but many were also tragically killed while venturing out onto the road of spreading the Gospel.

A beautiful piece that Scripture reveals is that Jesus, Himself, wept over death. In John chapter 11, Jesus stood outside of Lazarus' tomb and wept. He wept a death wail. He, the Son of God, through whom all things came into existence and apart from whom nothing has come into existence (John 1), knowing full well that He was going to raise Lazarus from the dead, wept right along with the mourning family. Perhaps He was weeping for those around Him whom He knew would not believe in Him even if He raised one from the dead: their fate, eternal damnation, a second death.

What we know for certain is what is written. After the wailing, Jesus removed the stone and cried out, "Lazarus, come forth." And yet there was still His greatest work to be done. Ed, in the midst of this dark solemn time clung to the Scriptures, to the Great Commission, "All authority has been given to Me in heaven and on earth. Go therefore and make disciples of all the nations, baptizing them in the name of the Father and the Son and the Holy Spirit, teaching them to observe all that I commanded you; and lo, I am with you always, even to the end of the age" (Matthew 28:18-20). He knew and trusted His Savior. Many would have been tempted to quit in response to the tragedy. Some would have used reasoning that sounded spiritual: "we were not meant to continue." Some would have spoken of signs. But not Ed. Thomas reports that Ed would not give up. He trusted in Jesus' authority. He believed that He would be with him. Thomas would go back to Grand Gedeh County. ACFI would not remain in a tomb.

One final note on the accident: one of the boys orphaned as a result of the accident—his mother having perished—came to live with Thomas and Tukutu. They took him in all those years ago.

It is not surprising that, years later, Thomas would go on to oversee the adoptions at the hands of the ACFI orphanage in its infancy. He believed in and participated in the adoption of orphans. Today, the boy from the accident is now a young man and still with Thomas and his wife, one of the seventeen in the tiny house outside Philadelphia.

9

"Where are you going?"

Life continued for the new ACFI missionaries. They continued in their work, patiently building a community of the faithful. In contrast, Samuel Doe's regime degraded and oppressed factions of his people. "The irrationality and cruelty of the Doe regime alienated much of the Liberian population, and frequent purges within the government and military created powerful enemies among the Liberian diaspora" (Lidow 150). As previously mentioned in Chapter five, the Quiwonkpa uprising led to Doe's brutal retribution. This brutality created many enemies abroad and paved the way for opportunistic warlord Charles Taylor to stage a rebellion of his own that led to one brutal rebel group rising out of the bloody ground after another. The civilian population helplessly lay at the mercy of the merciless.

Doe was unaware of the activities of Charles Taylor. On Christmas Eve in 1989, Taylor's rebel surge invaded Nimba County, where Cece's brother, Randolph was. The people of this county had suffered mercilessly as Doe had brutally suppressed the Quiwonkpa uprising and thrashed the civilian population in former years. It was madness all over again. "Government soldiers just started arresting people, accusing them of supporting the rebels," Thomas explained. "There arose a mentality that if you were not from Grand Gedeh then you were on the side of the rebellion. Those who are not for us are against us. No one was considered neutral." Thomas was thrown in jail again on some false charges. This time he knew he had to escape. They were killing people indiscriminately. He managed to free himself and arrange a ride out of the county on the back of a dirt bike. He eventually made it back to Monrovia to be with his wife and child.

Doe had increased the numbers and strengthened the security at the checkpoints across Liberia in an effort to contain the rebels. Taylor's newly formed group, the National Patriotic Front of Liberia (NPFL) quickly gained momentum, as previously mentioned in Chapter Five. "Town after town fell to the NPFL as Doe's soldiers withdrew from hostile territory. By late January the NPFL was pushing beyond Nimba County and advancing toward Monrovia and the coast...after two months, Prince Yormie Johnson, who had led the NPFL's first crossing into Liberia, broke from the group and formed the Independent NPFL (INPFL). Heavy fighting between the AFL (Doe) and NPFL (Taylor) provided cover for the small splinter faction, allowing it to travel fast and light through the bush, picking up recruits along the way" (Lidow 151). Ed and Cece were in the U.S. pleading for assistance. That's when Cece returned to Monrovia.

Thomas moved through the warring counties in an attempt to rescue his missionary brothers in Nimba and witnessed the "death wells" along the way. Holes deep and wide were filled with corpses of his countrymen: machete-hacked limbs and headless torsos, countless families ended, countless children orphaned. He later learned that his missionary brothers had escaped to the bush at the onslaught.

"By the end of June of 1990, Prince Johnson's troops had captured the western suburbs of Monrovia while the NPFL rapidly closed in from the north and east...Taylor proclaimed himself president of Greater Liberia and formed his own government. This government did not stand in the way of virtual ethnic cleansing of ethnic Krahn and Mandingo civilians by the NPFL soldiers. The Krahn and Mandingo were seen as collaborators with the Doe regime and were resented by many Liberians for the privileges and wealth that accrued to some Krahn and Mandingo under Doe's government" (Lidow 153).

The preceding details give the reader a glimpse of the hostile mindsets of the members of rebel factions and of how there was no end in sight to the bloodshed. Even the peacekeeping organization from the surrounding nations, the Economic Community of West African States (ECOWAS) that Doe called upon in desperation, would send its own military observer group (ECOMOG). But these soldiers also would go on to participate in looting and rapes and civilian abuses after Doe's death (Lidow 212). ECOMOG would go on to form alliances with other rising rebel factions (that have not been named in this writing) in a desperate attempt to defeat Charles Taylor's NPFL. These were all violent, brutal factions. The civilian population would suffer tremendously at the hands of each one. God had placed ACFI in the midst of astounding need. He gave great courage to Thomas Peters who would act as one of His agents amidst the carnage and chaos.

Monrovia choked on its rebels. Ed was in exile in Sierra Leone, and Cece and her children were stranded in a section that Thomas could not get to. Thomas says of that time, "You would trade the little clothing you had for food. I left my wife to go on a food finding mission. I left her at 8 months pregnant, weeping because she said the baby was no longer moving." On that day, he and a companion set out, knowing that they would all die soon if they came home empty-handed.

They walked along the crippled streets and saw a man standing in the middle of the street fifty feet or so ahead. "Where are you going?" he called to them, his hands behind his back. Thomas answered that they were looking for food. The man shook his head at them, slowly, and there rising from the scrub brush were rebels on either side of the road.

"This is an ambush," the man said to Thomas, revealing his automatic weapon from behind his back. "Walk on until you come to the next village, but do not turn back."

As they were ordered, Thomas and his friend started in the direction of the next village. The rebels watched them walk on, preventing them from reentering the city and warning others. But one of them emerged from the side and approached Thomas. After calling to him, he took him aside. Thomas recognized him as a boyhood playmate, one from Sierra Leone. They had played together in the streets as children.

"Do not go through the village," he warned. "Take the road straight ahead and do not veer off into the village."

The chief of the village would hold people who were passing through. This was the practice in many parts of Liberia and then Sierra Leone during their civil wars, Thomas explains. He would call a town meeting and ask for someone to give an account of the newcomer. It calls to mind the jungle justice implemented in the early years of Liberia. If no one stepped forward and claimed to know the person as family, then the person was shot dead. Everyone was suspect. The rebel who had ordered Thomas to the village was sending him to a certain death. And yet, by God's providence, another rebel saved Thomas' life.

The two traveled on knowing that this was the main highway leading to Sierra Leone. Behind them fighting erupted. They were forced to go forward or die, and he knew he was leaving behind Tukutu, uncertain of when he would see her again, uncertain that the baby she carried was alive. The way was not easy, a brutal trek.

The men concealed themselves by posing as workers traveling alongside Sierra Leone women. Thomas carried oversized, heavy suitcases on his head and on his back from one checkpoint to another. The group grew in numbers and rebels would tell them that some of them would have to die on the way, that there were too many of them to pass. The rebels didn't mind the Sierra Leone nationals leaving Liberia. They saw them as just going back home, Thomas says. He worked to blend in and held onto his identification card identifying him as a pastor.

Approaching one of the checkpoints, he saw bodies on the side of the road, gaping gunshot wounds and blood still wet and pooling. He and his companion, while walking, could not resist looking, their heads turning as they passed by. When they arrived, the commander of the checkpoint said to identify themselves. Thomas said, "I am a pastor," and showed him his identification card.

The commander waved his gun toward the dead men. "Do you see these men I just killed?" he asked, redirecting his gun at Thomas. "Tell me, Pastor, am I going to heaven or to hell?"

Thomas swallowed.

"Am I going to heaven or hell?!" the commander yelled.

"It all depends on what you choose now," Thomas began.

The commander moved the gun closer to Thomas' face.

"If you choose to go to hell, you can go to hell," Thomas continued, blood still pouring from the bodies nearby.

Over and over the rebel thrust the gun at Thomas' face and demanded an answer to his question, "AM I GOING TO HEAVEN OR HELL?!"

Thomas stood still, trembling inside, resisting the urge to look back at the bodies. "Not because you killed them will you go to hell," he answered. "You can ask for God's forgiveness. There is forgiveness for sins. Then you will not go to hell."

The commander lowered his weapon. He then said something so strange that as Thomas told of the man's remarks, they silenced us both for a few moments. "I thought you were going to lie to me and tell me that because I killed a man, I would go to hell." He paused, and added, "then I was going to kill you. I know what the Bible says about repentance and forgiveness for sins. I know you are a man of God. You can go." And the murderer waved them through.

The two managed to put one foot in front of the other and walk on though their hearts were still beating like a rabbit's.

What Thomas explains is that most of the time he did or said things he didn't know until after he was finished doing or saying them. This was the way it went, the most hideous of seasons— the brutal killings, the sadism and mass graves, the delirium from starvation and dehydration, the betrayals. Many felt that death was better than living.

Nights sleeping in open air followed by days with no food and little water left Thomas spent with fever. When he came to the final checkpoint, the last one before Sierra Leone, he could barely stand. The rebels kept the people there for a week before they would let them cross. Thomas grew sicker.

One night, gunfire and yelps of celebration erupted from a nearby town. Word traveled to those at the checkpoint that Prince Yormie Johnson, the rebel who was warring with Charles Taylor, had been captured in Monrovia. Jubilation filled the camp. As part of the celebration, they allowed everyone present to form a line to cross the bridge to their final destination. Thomas describes the line as so very, very long. He, in his illness, could not stand in it. It began to rain and then pour. The water pelted the low slung tin roof of a small building nearby making a strange music before it rolled to the ground. Thomas got out of the line and made his way to the shelter. He leaned against the outside wall. A rebel spotted him and moved towards him.

"Where are you going?!" he screamed close to Thomas' face.

"I am sick," Thomas weakly answered.

"You are trying to escape!" he accused.

"No, I am sick," Thomas repeated.

The rebel ordered Thomas to take off his clothing. Thomas knew that this was the procedure just before they killed a person. Thomas removed some of his clothing. Other rebels approached. They kicked him and slapped him on the ear. Thomas stood waiting to die.

From a short distance away another rebel called to the ones beating Thomas, summoning them away briefly. Thomas kept standing there, too ill to move. He thought it was better to die than to continue. He spoke to the Lord submitting to Him and telling Him he was at peace if this was the day He had chosen to take him home.

Another rebel appeared. "What are you doing here?"

"I am sick," Thomas panted.

He kicked at his clothes and Thomas' wallet fell out. He picked up the wallet and shuffled through its contents. The other rebels returned.

"Are you a pastor?" he asked holding the identification card.

Thomas nodded.

Someone ran at Thomas with a gun pointed at his face. The one holding the wallet stopped him. "Don't you know that this man is a pastor? Don't you know that the pastors protested against Doe, asking Doe to step down?"

Thomas knew about the peace march, the one that had led to Ed's exile. This one rebel had known about the appeal. The other rebels who had beaten Thomas received rebukes as well. All stood down.

Thomas was told to put on his clothing. Then the rebel who held his wallet escorted him to the front of the very long line of weary people. He walked him up and onto the bridge. As the two men stood on the bridge together in the rain, he pointed to the other side.

"Cross," he said to Thomas, and handed him his wallet and pastor identification.

Thomas says that in Bible school he read Scriptures about heaven. As a Sunday school teacher he taught children stories about heaven. In church services he heard preachers preach sermons about heaven, and when worshiping he sang songs about heaven. But on that day, at the crossing of that bridge, Thomas says, he felt he experienced heaven. Standing on the other side, totally free, he got down on his knees.

What Thomas revealed next is both amazing and deeply saddening. Merely ten minutes had passed after his crossing into Sierra Leone. The bridge was just behind him when he heard gunfire fill the air on the Liberian side. Prince Johnson had appeared on BBC television mocking Charles Taylor. The report that he had been killed in the attack was false, and the news had just reached this checkpoint. Thomas said that in the BBC clip, Johnson likened his escaping the assassination attempt to dancing to reggae music, each move allowing him to dodge the gunfire. Johnson mimicked his moves as he looked into the camera and laughed.

In retaliation, the rebels began slaughtering the civilians standing in line waiting to cross the bridge. Thomas could hear screams amidst the gunfire. People ran for their lives into the

Liberian bush, so close to their destination. A heavy-hearted Thomas continued on toward Freetown.

When he arrived in Freetown, he approached a police officer in hopes that if he spoke his father's name he would gain assistance in finding a place to stay. This woman knew of his father and took Thomas to where his half-brothers were. He stayed with them until he regained his strength.

There was no way to get in contact with Ed. Thomas was not even certain what country Ed was in, until one day when he decided to attend a soccer match and sat near a man who was cheering during the game. Thomas says that Liberians have a distinct way of rejoicing over a goal in a soccer match. This man rejoiced in this manner. Thomas approached him. It was Patrick, a member of the ACFI church.

Patrick was amazed and said that everyone thought Thomas was dead. The news was that he had been shot to death. Patrick had been in contact with Ed and gave Thomas Ed's contact number. When Ed heard Thomas' voice on the phone his first words were, "Where is my wife? Where are my children?"

10

In Perils of the Wilderness

"Ol' Ma, where is my father's wife so that I may take
her some food?"

So began a season in Thomas Peters' life of perilous treks
across treacherous ground. His first mission was given to him
by Ed himself, wrought out of his deep concern for the Church
in Monrovia. "Go and find the brothers and sisters who are
scattered. Gather them together for prayer and encouragement."
He gave Thomas money to buy them food. He also sent Thomas
to find Cece and the children and to deliver a bag of rice and
money for supplies.

Thomas set off, having secured a seat on an ECOMOG gun
boat. The boat was small and the waters choppy. He vomited
during the entire journey. The boat came to rest well off land as
the rebels launched rockets at them. They waited out of striking
distance in the water. The night was long and there came a quiet
opportunity to come ashore the next morning.

The city was frozen. It seemed nothing good moved, Cece
recalls. Nothing was turned over or replenished. "We were
dying," Cece says in her soft Liberian accent. "I was emaciated.

There was no money to buy food."

Hunger and cholera were squatters in every household. Ed Jr. had contracted cholera as an infant and by God's intervention survived. The dead rotted on streets amidst stagnant water and stagnant sewage. Scads of roving teenaged boys clung to their automatic weapons like small children cling to ice cream cones. They gathered in packs in open-bed trucks and moved through the street like a storm surge in slow motion. Piercing eyes. Piercing empty bellies. Cece recalls venturing out into a crowd, half out of her mind with hunger and desperation for her children, when a truckload of rebels swerved over and into the pedestrians, killing some. She was struck and flew into the air, her slippers still on the ground. Someone delivered her to the hospital in a wheelbarrow. She miraculously survived.

On one of these many days in her wilderness she sat on the front stoop, staring, no longer batting at the flies. A man approached on foot, pausing in front of her.

"Ol' Ma," he raised his chin to her, "where is my father's wife so I may take her some food?"

She found it hard to speak through her dry mouth and swollen tongue.

"Ol' Ma," he repeated.

Cece recalls looking at him in disbelief. She strained to focus. They had all thought he was dead. But here he was, calling to her, her beloved Thomas Peters. In utter amazement she answered, "Wleh Peters, it is me."

His expression did not change, and she could see that he did not recognize her all bones and sunken eyes.

"Now, why are you lying to me, Ol' Ma," he said in an agitated tone. "Tell me where my father's wife is so I may take her some food!"

"Wleh Peters," she said again. "It's me, Cece."

A look of horror came over the courageous young man's face. Cece will never forget that her spiritual son did not know her by sight. He then made his way closer, stood over her and showed her the bag of rice. He told her he brought money from Ed to buy food. Cece began to cry.

> *I have made you, and I will carry you;*
> *I will sustain you, and I will rescue you.*
> *(Isaiah 46:4)*

Thomas found Tukutu, by God's grace, and their four year old daughter, standing in the street. They saw one another and Tukutu rejoiced! "I thought you were dead!" she said, laughing and crying. Thomas embraced her, but his daughter would not come to him. "She did not know who I was," Thomas says, shaking his head. "It had been too long since she had seen me." Knowing his wife and daughter were alive and learning that his Tukutu had survived a late-term miscarriage at the outbreak of war, Thomas was certain God was sustaining his family. After securing them in a home with other church members and giving them provisions, he went to work.

He found a dear ACFI brother named Sackie, and together they sought out the ACFI church leaders, gathered them together and gave them money from Ed to buy food. They encouraged one another and strengthened one another. They witnessed to one another of God's good hand in their lives and of His provisions. Thomas knew he had to get Cece out of Liberia and into Sierra Leone to be reunited with her husband. But Cece refused to go until she knew her children were taken care of. They had all scattered, except for the infant and the twin toddlers. Lucy, she had reported to Thomas, had been taken by the rebels.

Thomas went to work searching for Ed's children. He found one, wandering the streets as if insane, an open wound on his leg. He was able to locate medication to treat the wound. He continued day in and day out gathering Ed's children from different parts of the city. He secured a house on the beach for them on the ACFI compound.

From there, Thomas began orchestrating his plans for evacuating Cece from Liberia. He journeyed back to Sierra Leone to connect with Ed. Thomas has expressed how difficult it would be to lead a ministry when one's family is in peril. He had always felt that by being one of the ones taking care of Ed's family, he was instrumental in keeping the ministry going. He gave Ed the news: almost all of his children were gathered. His wife was secure.

The borders were now closed. They were accepting no more Liberian refugees into Sierra Leone. Thomas and Ed approached a member of the new Sierra Leone ACFI church. They asked him to pose as Cece's husband and father to their young children and to accompany them into Sierra Leone. This would be a most dangerous mission as the mode of travel was by a

Nigerian gun boat. The man's withered hand was evidence that he was not exactly soldier material. He bravely accepted the mission. Papers were fabricated and Cece and three of her young children were delivered safely to Ed in Sierra Leone, thanks to this crippled Moses and his great God. They would not be separated again until Ed would bring Cece to the United States.

At this time during the war, all the children were accounted for and cared for. All except for one.

11

"I will come to you"

(John 14:8b)

The rebels, Thomas explains, were separated into splinter factions under different commanding officers. It was organized chaos. At checkpoints, the rebels acted more or less brazenly depending on who was their commanding officer. "My C.O. is higher than your C.O.!" they screamed at fellow rebels attempting to pass through and confiscate their weapons or vehicles. Widespread drug use inflated their impetuous tempers.

"I had to act bigger than they were, more important and never afraid," Thomas says. "Inside I might be shaking, but I must never show it."

He had heard of a place in the interior where the rebels kept the captured females. Making it out of the city would be difficult enough, but to find transportation to the interior required a plan. At the St. Paul Bridge, many different kinds of people still came together to trade goods for food. Thomas studied their system for some time. In this setting he could begin on one side of the bridge posing as a merchant and slip to the other side when the market was shutting down, posing as a rebel. He set his prices high so as not to run out of goods too quickly. As the day drew to a close he lowered his prices drastically and off-loaded all his goods. Slipping into a baseball cap and sagging his shorts in teen-aged fashion, he arose with a swagger on the other side.

Some rebels were loading wares onto a vehicle and Thomas told them he wanted to go to Tubmanburg. The driver charged Thomas for a seat. As more passengers piled in Thomas was pushed out of his seat and forced to stand. With only his left foot planted on the floorboard he gripped the roof rack with both hands.

They arrived at night. Thomas was exhausted. He wanted to connect with a friend in the area but didn't know the way to his home in Josephtown. A group of women sat together nearby. Asking for directions would draw attention to himself, and he knew they would then ask him where he was from. As he contemplated, one of them called to him, "What kind of a lazy soldier are you? Why do you just stand there looking like that? Even if you are so tired you could just walk there to Josephtown." She pointed in the direction of a stop light in the near distance. The other women laughed at him.

Upon his arrival to Josephtown Thomas connected with his old friend who was quite ill. He spent a restless night there and resumed his mission the next morning. He approached a man in town to ask where he could find young women to accompany him. The man directed him to the place he was looking for and upon arriving amongst the young girls, he was careful to keep a distance from the one he thought was Lucy. "I didn't want her to see me and cry out my name or jump on me in excitement," he says. He had another male approach her and say her name, telling her there was someone from Monrovia who wanted to talk to her.

Convincing her to come with him would be hard, Thomas explains. They used lies and fear to control their captives. The girls were convinced that all the members of their families were dead and there was no one left in Monrovia. They thought this was the only place where they would find food and shelter and believed the rest of Liberia had been destroyed in the war. He decided to use the United States as a lure. "All Liberians long to go to the United States. They think of it as heaven. I knew if I told her that her family was alive and we were all going to the United States that she would come with me."

Thomas had obtained a pass as a soldier. Armed with multiple passes, identification cards, and money from Ed, he paid a captive's ransom, and he and Lucy escaped. Together they started on their week-long trek back to Monrovia.

Utterly bizarre and stranger-than-fiction events occurred along the way. He was clearly not alone but accompanied by a heavenly army. How else could one man of modest stature single-handedly deliver a stolen girl to her family through fields of enemies? The answer resides in Thomas' God. We do not know the reason that He saved Lucy and spared Thomas. We know that it was only possible through Him. Thomas demonstrated great faith, great courage and great determination. God demonstrated His power and mercy. At checkpoint after checkpoint violent rebels confronted Thomas threatening to end his mission, but Thomas always gave the same answer in a steady, calm voice:

"I am on a mission from the Highest Commander."

"Who is your commanding officer?" they screamed into his unblinking eyes.

"My commander is the Highest Commander," he said over and over, the rebels not knowing he spoke of the LORD of Hosts. It is written of Him: "He who reduces rulers to nothing, who makes the judges of the earth meaningless" (Isaiah 40:23).

Checkpoint after checkpoint, he was allowed to pass through with Lucy. Two children of the Most High God, exposed, but not alone, moved through the most violent battlegrounds of the earth.

"Faith in God alone is key," Ed says. Thomas had listened and learned well from his mentor.

It is not my intention to convey to the reader that this week-long trek was not brutal. The fact that they made it back alive could only be through God's provision. To the rebels, they were nameless faces easy to eliminate. They molested, tortured, raped, castrated, mutilated, and murdered daily and readily. There were no limits to the violence. Thomas and Lucy both endured abuse along the way. But the purpose of this book is not to spend time there. We must acknowledge that apart from Christ, we all are capable of great evil. Every time Thomas called on His God as the Highest Commander, every opportunity he seized to give honor to His name in the face of death, God was glorified. He rewarded Thomas with his life, as He says in the book of Jeremiah, *"but I will give your life to you as a prize in all places where you may go" (Jeremiah 45:5b).*

And so it was that this part of their wilderness was over. Lucy was reunited with her brothers and sisters.

12

The Church Between Two Chapters

In God's providence, any situation may be used to draw people to Himself. This small section of the book, although only taking up space between two chapters, is both deep and wide in significance.

Before Lucy was rescued and while Ed was still in Sierra Leone caring for two of his small children, Cece was recovering in the United States. Ed heard a report that his precious daughter Lucy was in a refugee camp in Nigeria. It was 1991. He boarded a plane with his two young sons to go and search for her, wanting desperately to recover his daughter for his beloved wife.

In the Liberian refugee camps in Nigeria he exhausted all leads and disproved the rumor. Heart-broken, he returned to Sierra Leone with his two children but in the airport was not permitted to reenter the country. While he had been traveling, the president of Liberia had made an agreement with the president of Sierra Leone that no Liberians would be allowed back into Sierra Leone, since the population in Liberia was dwindling. Ed's two children were taken from him. He had no money to pay anyone for assistance. He was forced back onto the airplane and flown back to Nigeria. His children remained in custody in Sierra Leone.

Security in Nigeria had tightened as well. He was apprehended in the airport and taken to jail for having no Nigerian paperwork and no money. For three days he prayed and waited from behind bars. *What was God doing to him?* He agonized. *WHAT ARE YOU DOING TO ME?!* He cried toward heaven like a Jeremiah. He could hardly allow himself to think of his two sons in Sierra Leone without their father and what this would do to Cece. Desperate and helpless, he persevered in prayer.

A man came to the jail and overheard Ed in conversation and identified him as Liberian by his accent.

"What are you doing here?" he asked Ed.

Ed explained who he was and his situation.

"You are a pastor," the man repeated with an open smile. He then paid Ed's bail, provided lodging for him at a nearby hotel and gave him money to sustain him.

Day in and day out Ed remained in this room praying. The cleaning teams would knock, peer in and enter. They changed his bed linens, wiped the sink, quietly moved about the room and around Ed. Finally, one worker asked him why he never left the room.

"I am a pastor..." Ed began, and told him of his situation.

In response to his reply, a steady stream of Nigerian men and women came to him for prayer. They shared the news with each other of the pastor in their midst. Shift after shift, they knocked on his door. Sometimes they would come alone, sometimes in groups—servants unseen to most people but not unseen to God.

Ed was an answer to many of their prayers. They were in

need of a shepherd. Ed interceded for them and taught them of Christ, the Good Shepherd.

One of the women asked if Ed would accompany her home, a long distance. He went. Many of her family members and friends greeted him as he entered her living room. They came to hear the preacher and to have him pray for them. In that very home, the ACFI church in Nigeria was founded. It remains to this day.

13

In Weariness and Toil

The Lord allowed Ed an opportunity to return to Sierra
Leone from Nigeria. A door was briefly opened and Ed slipped
through it. He gathered his two children and brought them back
to Liberia, but he then had to hurry to the United States to tend
to his wife who was in need of medical attention. Lucy had been
delivered out of the hands of the rebels and into the hands of
her family, and Ed and Cece were so grateful. But they were still
a fractured family. Ed entered into a season of moving back and
forth between the United States, Liberia, Nigeria, and Sierra
Leone.

Back and forth. In and out. Here and there. All the while, the
rebels changed names and faces and allegiances, but not tactics.
War is hell, and many of Ed's children remained in the middle
of it. During these next few years Ed would confess his
weariness, his longing to be in one place and reunited
permanently with his dear wife, and his overwhelming feelings
of helplessness. But, however he may have felt, his actions were
faithful and constant. He continued to minister to the needs of
the most destitute: sharing provisions as containers arrived
from churches in the United States, teaching and training
pastors to bring the Gospel to his suffering countrymen, and

supporting the churches in Sierra Leone and Nigeria, just to name a few.

Brother Peters, as Ed refers to Thomas, remained in Liberia providing parental guidance and protection for Ed's children. In April 1996, he would be called upon again to play the role of rescuer during the worst fighting yet to come.

But before we enter into the next set of stories, let us stop here and take note of the beginnings of the orphanages.

When Thomas and Ed's children were stable at the ACFI compound in Monrovia, Ed was overseeing ministries in Liberia and other African countries, traveling sometimes to tend to his wife and small children in the United States. Thomas reports that in Monrovia children were everywhere. "They would come to the lunchtime ministry once we set it up at the compound and they wouldn't leave. They would just hang around all night long." Busloads of children would arrive from the interior where many had witnessed the violent murders of their parents. Malnourished, stunned, terror-stricken children waited for food and shelter.

This is how the ACFI orphanage began. A raw need was placed at the disciples' feet and they met the need. The first orphanage was established at the ACFI headquarters on the beaches of Monrovia. The adoption piece would soon follow. Ed felt it made sense that these traumatized children would be best served in loving homes, and so ACFI would begin to support adoption as part of their caring for the children. Let the reader recall this when reading the later chapter titled, "In Perils of False Brethren." Remember how the children came to be gathered into an orphanage, and also remember the hearts of the men and women who put their hands to the plow and did not forsake them.

Currently there are just under 150 children in the ACFI orphanage located in Dixville—the Daniel Hoover Village— many of whom are boarding students during the school year. During the Ebola outbreak of 2014 they were safely quarantined on the campus along with the children from the school for the Deaf. They safely awaited the eradication of the Ebola virus which plagued West Africa. Although the civil war is now over, ACFI is still in the business of children. And Ed, still weary from traveling back and forth, gathers support and supplies to send to the ministers on the ground and to the children depending on him. Loading containers with bags of rice purchased with the money God provides, ordering medications from American missions relief organizations, writing letters, gathering, prayer...toil is not a word that is, in reality, suitable, but weariness surely applies.

14

In Perils in the Sea

*Greater love has no one than this, than one
lay down his life for his friends
(John 15:13)*

His name was Jackson.

Jackson loved Romeo.

And Romeo loved the blind men.

In the fall of 1995, Ed and Cece's oldest living son, Jackson, was 21 years of age. He was thoughtful and sincere, a most responsible young man; the kind of young man who carefully placed his feet in the footprints his father left in the sand. Everyone assumed he would one day step into a leadership position in the ACFI church. He was already assuming a servant-leader's role in ministry.

Earlier that year, fighting had spread to over 80 percent of Liberia's territory. Civilians suffered extremely. The number of Liberian refugees swelled to nearly 800,000 (Lidow 159). The worst was yet to come in April of 1996 when Charles Taylor's NPFL would form an alliance with a former enemy in an attempt to wipe out Taylor's greatest threat to his power, another rebel, Roosevelt Johnson, the leader of ULIMO-J. At this time, though, there were attempts to establish a transitional government to include members from warring factions.

ACFI went about its business. On the Oceanview compound, more newly-orphaned children arrived. They were nursed, fed and introduced to the church. Once stable, they were transferred to one of the satellite orphanages. Food and medical supplies were distributed. Water from the hand-dug well was pumped and shared with any and all who came and asked. The blind men were cared for and their faith nourished by the ACFI servants. Romeo, Ed's nephew, tended to menial tasks on the compound. It was just another day in war-torn Monrovia. A hot sunny day. A day that could tempt one to a swim.

Swimming in this part of the Atlantic Ocean is far different from American eastern seaboard swimming. Perhaps Romeo wanted to take a sabbatical from the years of war and behave as a normal teenager. Perhaps he wanted to remind himself that he was still a child. On this particular day in the fall of 1995 he stripped off his shirt and ran out to the sea, leaping over the waves, his body then cutting through the crests. With arms like a windmill he went farther and farther away from shore.

A riptide caught him and he began to struggle. Ed recalls being on the compound but unaware that Romeo was in the water. Jackson, seeing his cousin and knowing for certain he would be lost at sea, dove into the ocean and darted for Romeo. Hand over head, he caught up to him. With little strength remaining he wrapped himself around Romeo and pulled him in the direction of the shore until Romeo was free of the current. Romeo found his feet and made it safely to shore. But Jackson. Oh, Jackson. His strength had been spent for another. A current came for him and, as quickly as Romeo had been released, Jackson was caught. He was carried out to sea so swiftly no one could save him. Gone. Screaming people watched helplessly from the shore. Gone. And Ed, alerted by the screaming came running to the beach hearing what all were saying and seeing their pointing fingers. Looking for his son. Looking out to sea. In perils of the sea, Ed's son was gone. In perils of the sea, Jackson traded his life for another. But the story does not end there. This is only the beginning. Ed's agony. His son. *Oh, my son.* He is gone. And Romeo on the shore, his head in his hands, saved.

As we have seen how Jackson loved Romeo, let us now see how Romeo loved the blind men. To know the blind men, we must pause and read a passage from the journal that a pastor of our church here in Tacoma penned on his first visit to Liberia. He had come to Liberia in response to one of Ed's journeys to the United States. Having listened to this man of faith, he decided along with the elders of the church to take a first-hand look at ACFI's endeavors. Pastor Bruce and others had come to teach and to train, but, as God often reverses the order of things, the teacher became the student. He writes:

"The evening meeting was designed as an evangelistic service. Steve Jones [one of the Americans] was the main speaker. He had prepared to talk about the first convert from Africa, the Ethiopian eunuch. Good call, Steve. But in spite of Steve's fine preaching, the thing that stuck in my mind from this service was the singing of eight young men who entered the building waving white canes in front of them. They were led to seats in the right-front corner. Now I'll say more later about African worship. It wouldn't surprise you to know that the singing of all the Africans we met was vocally exuberant and animated by joyful dance. This is exactly what we observed for the first 20 minutes. But then it was time for the Echoes of the Blind choir to sing a cappella.

"Here were men who existed on the lowest rung of their humiliated, impoverished society. They'd been taunted and beaten because of their obvious defenselessness. Recently their landlord had kicked them out of their one small room where twenty of them lived a crowded and meager existence. But God through ACFI provided a gutted-out house for them to live in, with one caregiver. They had come on a Saturday night to communicate their gratefulness to a loving God.

"I was about to learn one of the unique ways God was maintaining joy in the hearts of wounded Liberians. He was using these men—who would have been suffering with or without the war—to sing His song to people who counted themselves entirely fortunate beside their blind brothers. I regard it as one of the chief privileges of my five decades to have been in the same room with these men on the night they confessed God's goodness before His people. Standing among a company of black worshippers, my white hands lifted to the sky, I heard the Echoes of the Blind sing words only God Himself could have taught them. "I still have joy. I still have joy. After all that I have been through, I still have joy."

"I observed many tears besides my own. It was rare to see

these war-toughened Africans weep. But God had planted a blessing among them that showed how precious they were to Him; so precious that He would mysteriously allow these eight singing men to bear their blindness in order that they in turn might touch the hearts of countless Liberians who otherwise might have suffered a handicap worse than blindness: the handicap of hardness. Liberians could also see in these men that real joy is possible even if your condition in this life has little prospect of changing. Their hope need not be attached to an expectation that their national nightmare would end. Here was unearthly joy. I personally have rarely felt so loved by God.

"I observed the rich earnestness in the faces of these shabby, sightless men. Some wore dark glasses, some did not. Like most blind performers, they had no self-consciousness about how they looked when they sang. The shortest tenor scrunched his eyes, as if squeezing out the high notes with his facial muscles. A paragon of determination. The lead singer maintained a serious, although not unpleasant, expression, the look of a man in charge. And they followed him with precision. For some reason, my favorite was a short guy with a lop-sided mouth. The louder he sang, the more his mouth would open, wide and round, but mainly on one side of his face. And if the crescendo increased, he would turn his head sideways and slightly upwards so the most open part of his mouth faced the audience. Call me crazy, but I loved that dear look. Unknowingly, he communicated that nothing else in the world mattered at that moment.

"I witnessed the uplifting effect these men had on Liberians. One of the seminar attendees, a single man named Aaron, wrote the following on his survey: 'My toughest challenge in the last twelve months is to hear of the death of my mother who has been praying for my salvation and has not seen the result of her prayer but only heard. With this news I was broken hearted and this caused a slowdown on me in the ministry work. In this period of slowdown, I heard and see some blind boys and a girl singing a song entitled, 'I still have joy, yet for all I have been through, I still have joy.' From this song I was moved and revived in the work of the Lord'" (pages 23 and 24).

This same journal introduces us to Romeo, his heart and his hand. Our pastor describes, on his ten day long visit in March 1996, his roommate getting up in the middle of the night having been awakened by a typical torrential downpour. The water battering the metal roof served as a kind of an alarm, a call to wake up and to come and see something remarkable. The roommate got out of bed and made his way through the dark quarters and to the door to the outside. He stopped and wept for the sight before him. There slept Romeo, lying on the cold stone tile floor, his body pressing up against the door with a friend. They had been barricading the door every night of these precious visitors' stay, putting themselves in harm's way, using their earthly bodies as a shield to guard against intruding rebels.

And what of Romeo loving the blind men? Just a few days later, during the hideous April 1996 rise in violence and slaughter of civilians, a marauding gang of rebels stopped at the ACFI compound. Jackson was with the Lord. The blind men were on the beach. These thugs descended upon the blind, forcing them to lie in the sand. They proceeded to terrorize them by firing bullets in between each one of them, going from one to another. The dear brother Pastor Bruce had written of, the one with the lop-sided mouth singing the Lord's song, how his face must have been contorted in his terror. These men without sight endured the piercing sounds of the bullets and the vibrations of them hitting the ground. Were they writhing in fear and yet fighting to hold so very still so as not to be hit? Did they imagine their dear brothers were being pierced with every pop? Wild laughter and pops alerted Romeo. He rushed to the scene and alone stood in between the rebels and the blind, demanding the horror cease. In Romeo fashion he used his body as a shield for the blind men. In a culture where those with special needs are discarded and seen as less than human, Romeo valued their lives above his own. He used his body as a barricade for these precious visitors; visitors to earth, citizens of heaven.

Later they found Romeo's dismembered body strewn across the sand, savagely murdered with a machete. Romeo is now with his Maker and his cousin. The people that loved him picked up the pieces. The blind men were spared and are still singing, even today, of the joy of the Lord.

For those who wonder of our God's intimate direction and involvement in our lives, written below as part of the closing to this piece is one of the final excerpts from our pastor's journal:

"I'd brought along a KJV Bible just in case all our students were using the old version. This particular Bible had been given to me by the seminary when I graduated, an especially thin edition that could be taken on hospital visits. I knew this Bible could be very useful to one of the leaders who had no Bible at all. I went down the darkened hall, searching for someone who had no Bible. The first person I ran into was Romeo. No, he didn't have a Bible. 'Here's one I don't want to take home with me. If you will use it, it's yours.' I decided not to tell him the background of this Bible for fear that he would refuse to take something of such perceived importance to me. I was delighted it was going to this particular young man. Four years before, he had watched as rebels shot his father (who was a pastor) for having the wrong T-shirt in his belongings. It was Romeo who hauled our water, cleaned our toilets and swept our floors on his hands and knees with a handful of straw. Then I said, 'Romeo, I want you to realize that your dad would be very proud of you now. I will be most blessed if my three sons grow up to be as faithful a servant as you are" (page 65).

A final note: Cece, Jackson's mother, was in the United States when Jackson died in the fall of 1995. She would not be able to return to Liberia until 1998. There was something about touching down in her home land, embracing her children she had been separated from for years, but no Jackson. It was as though she had lost Jackson all over again. It was almost as though he had just drowned.

Jesus said to her, "I am the resurrection and the life; he who
believes in Me will live even if he dies, and everyone who lives
and believes in Me will never die. Do you believe this?"
(John 11:25-26)

15

April 6, 1996

The worst phase of the war. As previously noted, Charles Taylor's NPFL formed an alliance with another rebel faction. The two forces attempted to arrest Roosevelt Johnson, Taylor's main opponent at his headquarters in Monrovia. "Krahn fighters (affiliated with the deceased Samuel Doe) came to Johnson's aid, and Monrovia descended into some of the worst violence of the war. Fighting in the city center carried on for weeks as gunmen preyed upon civilians and half of Monrovia's swollen population of 1.3 million fled their homes" (UNSC 1996b as cited by Lidow 161).

In January of 1996, only three months prior, Ed's mother Lacy Kofi had been released from seven years of rebel captivity in her village. She had just come into Monrovia and was killed in the crossfire by rebel fighters during the April violence. Ed's agony multiplied. After Romeo's brutal murder, rebels seized and occupied the ACFI headquarters. God would provide ACFI soldiers of Christ in addition to Ed's dear sister Susie to save Ed's children. Thomas Peters' story is recorded below.

First, Thomas escorted the blind men, taking them from the headquarters to Mother Buchanan's (Cece's aunt's) home and then to another home in New Kru Town, out of the hot zone.

He and other brave ACFI leaders would move the orphans who were still at the headquarters to a safer location. Ed's father was distraught and paralyzed with grief in response to his wife's murder. Thomas carted him to safety in a wheelbarrow. With bullets whizzing by, bombs lighting up the streets and rebels upon rebels fighting on behalf of their warlords, Thomas moved through the city dressed as one of them, posturing as a commanding officer, often barreling down gripped streets in a vehicle with its flashers on. When Ed's mother's body was taken to JFK Hospital, Thomas feared her body would be cremated with other incoming casualties. Thomas employed his sister who worked at JFK to assist him in securing the body so that it would be preserved for a proper burial upon Ed's arrival. She was, after all, Ed's mother. It was in response to the April violence that Thomas helped move Ed's children from Monrovia to Sierra Leone where they would remain until it became too dangerous even there. He would have to find the courage, again, to aid them in that dangerous situation. But that is a later chapter.

The April 6 violence brought Ed into another time of desperation; another time where his God would reach down from heaven and spare his life with His provisions.

16

In Hunger and In Thirst

(still within the April 6 surge in violence)

"Do you have anything to eat today, Ed?"
"Sweet tea. I have sweet tea. Bless the Lord."

Panic. An entire city inflamed and full of refugees displaced from years of terror at the hands of rebels in the interior, fell into utter chaos and panic. Merciless mercenaries slaughtered civilians, and people headed for the only place that they saw as a safe haven: the U.S. embassy. Surely there they would find protection. Like blood rushing through the veins to the lungs for oxygen, the people rushed through the streets toward the embassy compound, running for their lives. Tens of thousands of Liberian bodies and souls crammed themselves onto the few acres of U.S. soil in the midst of Monrovia: a walled section called Greystone.

Ed's health was failing. A hepatitis virus that affected his liver was taking its toll on his exhausted, malnourished body. Since he had refused to go with Thomas and the others to a safer northwest suburb, he was now caught in the city's panic. He recalls that death became almost visible to him. He waited until dusk and then fled for the embassy compound.

U.S. Marines closed the gate as the grounds were dangerously packed with civilians. Armed guards surrounded Greystone, letting no one else in. Exposed and cut off, Ed surveyed his surroundings. An old woman huddled on the ground on the side of the road unable to get up and move while others passed her by. Ed saw her and moved toward her. Then, hoisting her onto his back, he steadied himself and darted for the gate, running through the crowded street, running with the old woman on his back, his arms behind him bracing her legs, her chin banging against his shoulder as her head jolted up and down with his strides. Some guards looked in their direction. In Ed's words, God confused them, and they started shouting, "Open the gate! Open the gate! Let the Ol' Ma in!" They pointed their guns in the air and opened the gate. "Let the Ol' Ma in! Let the Ol' Ma in!"

Inside the walled field, there were no buildings, only grass and large rocks here and there. Thousands were spread across the lot. The sanitation was horrible. Ed squeezed through the crowd and gently set the woman on the ground. The rain pelted them as they huddled so tightly packed together, old and young, men and women. Some held onto live chickens. Many had babies swaddled on their backs. Ed knew that if one impetuous rebel fired into this crowd there would be certain panic and death for many, both by gunfire and trampling. He grieved for them and pressed his way through, making his way to an exit that opened onto Broad Street.

Faith in God alone is key.

With sallow, sickly eyes he looked up and down the street. Thomas Peters told years later of his sulfur-yellow eyes. The jaundice that marked Ed's body at this time. He had very little strength, his body plagued with hepatitis. He wondered if he would live through this phase of the war as he stood on Broad Street in the relentless rain.

A young man appeared and spoke to Ed. He worked for the newspaper and explained that he had access to the building the newspaper company owned. Once inside the building Ed not only found a place to rest but he also found a working telephone. He phoned the pastor of our church and his wife, among others, calling on them to pray. Consider yet another of the Lord's sustaining interventions on Ed's behalf. For as the rain continued to fall, relentless and pelting, Ed, who had no food or water or money for provisions, began collecting the rainwater into containers that he set out in the courtyard of this newspaper building. For two weeks he was holed up in this building and this "water" he collected was all that he had to eat or drink. But what Ed reports is that the rainwater did not taste like mere water but tasted like tea, sweet and sustaining.

When Ed would call our pastor to let him know he was still alive, our pastor asked, "Have you had anything to eat today, Ed?" And Ed would answer, "Sweet tea. I have sweet tea. Bless the Lord." This was no ordinary water. But that is not the end of this portion of the story. For while God was sustaining Ed with what Ed described as sweet tea, God was weaving together a plan of rescue in another faithful follower. Wayne Shenk was a bold Canadian missionary who had partnered with Ed and ACFI in spreading the Gospel in Liberia before our Tacoma church's partnership. While Ed held on, Wayne worked on a plan to deliver provisions to Ed that would enable him to escape and also provide vital nutrients to strengthen Ed's body. Many speak of Joseph's amazing coat of many colors. Ed would be handed an amazing coat of his own.

Drip down, Oh heavens, from above, and let the clouds pour down righteousness; let the earth open up and salvation bear fruit, and righteousness spring up with it.
I, the LORD, have created it.
(Isaiah 45:8)

In Canada, half a world away, Wayne's dear mother stitched and sewed not a coat of many colors, but a coat of many compartments. As though it were out of an espionage movie, Wayne and his mother devised a plan to alter a winter vest by ripping the seams apart and replacing the feathery down with containers filled with bundles of cash and vitamins. In times past, Ed had called on Wayne to travel to the outskirts of Liberia teaching of the God of the Bible, bringing the good news of salvation through Jesus Christ. Many ACFI pastors loved Wayne. His love for the Liberian people was evident in his actions. He would not shrink back during the heightened violence of the wars. He would exemplify such bravery, and God would honor it by allowing him success in his mission. Amazingly, by God's Providence, Wayne was able to find a way in.

Westerners were being evacuated out of Liberia. None were allowed in. By faith, Wayne decided to make his way to Sierra

Leone, close enough, and then pray that the Lord would provide a way into Liberia from there. Once in Sierra Leone Wayne made his way to the Lungi Airport. He stood at a safe distance clasping his bundle, a backpack containing the vest. He observed, through a fence, helicopters taking off and landing, U.S. Marines executing evacuations of westerners out of Monrovia. Helicopters would leave empty and come back filled, offloading desperate people who had escaped a sort of hell on earth. Wayne, desperate to get in, broke through the marine-guarded opening and reached a pilot, pleading with him to deliver his bundle to the U.S. aid office in Monrovia. He knew that any vehicle donning an American flag could travel throughout Liberia unhindered. Liberians still had such faith in America. He asked the pilot to employ an aid worker to deliver this pack to a man at the newspaper building. This is very difficult to imagine in the economy of a war: one man delivering a backpack containing a vest to another in a capital that was collapsing. But Wayne begged, his arm extended, and the airman accepted.

Upon arrival in Monrovia, the pilot delivered the backpack containing the supplies to a worker at the U.S. aid office and in a vehicle donning the American flag delivered it to the newspaper office where Ed was holed up. Wayne had communicated with Ed via the landline to dismantle the seams of the vest. Ed tore apart the vest and found the cans of vitamins. Concealed beneath the vitamins and wrapped tightly into bundles was $25,000.

Ed had provisions for food and vitamins for healing.

Charles Taylor along with the rebel factions aligned with him sealed their position as the dominant power. Groups returned to the negotiating table. Disarmament began. In July 1997, elections were held. Charles Taylor won in a landslide victory (Lidow 161).

17

More Perils in the Wilderness

In May of 1997, Ed's children, who had been evacuated from Monrovia during the April 1996 violence, were then in peril as Liberian refugees in Sierra Leone. One man, Charles Taylor, seemed to be igniting fires beneath Ed's children's beds wherever they slept. During the time of cementing his dominance in Liberia, he promoted war in Sierra Leone, looted the mines for diamonds and funneled Liberian rebels loyal to him into Sierra Leone to fight alongside the rebels there. The more unstable the region, the more sure he was of holding onto power. Liberians were despised in their neighboring countries, seen as war mongers by neutral civilians and those loyal to their own governments. And Ed's children were caught up in the middle of it.

Thomas learned of their deteriorating situation while he was in Monrovia. He devised a plan to move Ed's children and some of the ACFI members from Sierra Leone to Guinea, the country north of Sierra Leone, yet another wilderness to them. Ed had flown back to the United States to tend to his wife and small children's medical needs. He sent $3,000 to Thomas as provisions to evacuate his children. Thomas hid the cash in the soles of an old pair of bathroom slippers, having split apart the thick platforms. After repairing the soles, he dragged them through the gravel to conceal the repair marks. He dressed simply, wearing casual cotton clothes and boots.

Next he had to get to the children. He knew that as a Liberian he would not be able to cross into Sierra Leone. Instead, he planned to approach Sierra Leone from Guinea. On the flight to Guinea from Monrovia, he met a man who invited him to stay the night at his home in Conakry, the capital. Seven men slept on the floor of this man's one-room shanty. Overcome with exhaustion, Thomas stepped over their bodies, tossed his shower slippers to the side, and joined them face down on the hard floor, hands drawn into his chest.

"My whole life was in those slippers," Thomas says. He knew that without the money he would not be able to buy their way through the checkpoints that littered the land.

The next morning his host escorted him to the border and approached a man who was taking people into Sierra Leone. But Thomas' Liberian accent was thick, he says, despite his attempts to soften it. The man refused to take him. A rebel caught sight of him and summoned him. He was made to strip off his clothes, and he did so down to his boots. They were looking for money, Thomas says, but they had tossed his slippers to the side before they began searching his body. The slippers lay on the ground nearby wearing Thomas' heart. Other than the frayed slippers, Thomas' only other valuable possession was a nice pair of boots, brown and leather, good for comfort and protection considering the amount of walking and traveling he was accustomed to. He began refastening his clothing when the checkpoint guard took a sudden interest in the boots.

"What are you wearing?" he asked eyeing his boots.

Thomas looked down.

"Take them off and give them to me," the guard commanded. Then he pointed his gun at Thomas and Thomas heard the click click click as the guard toyed with his nerves. He didn't want to speak and have his Liberian accent give him away. He knew they were just killing Liberians. Inside he was trembling, but he gathered his courage and stared into the clicking gun.

"You got a small gun," he chided. "You know what I deal with? I deal with 66 calibers. The one you got is small," Thomas sneered.

Thomas knew the way they thought. The ones with bigger anything and more of anything must be commanding officers. The bluff worked, praise be to God. Of course, anyone who knows anything about guns knows that there is no such thing as 66 calibers. "I was speaking of the 66 books of the Bible," Thomas says all these years later...and then smiles.

When he arrived in Freetown, he sent for the children. They chartered a minivan and set out, armed with the money stowed in the shower slippers. He knew the journey would be brutal, and so he warned them all. Such perils these tender souls endured. What should have been a four-hour drive took two long days. At every checkpoint they were forced out of the van and were often stripped. Their accusers searched for the Liberian rebel brand marks on their bodies as well as for money or valuables. Of course none of these bodies bore the brandings. But these soldiers would separate Thomas from the others, separate them one from another and take them into the dark, into empty spaces. When they returned, the girls were visibly rattled and grieved. The shower slippers were always dropped to the side as Thomas was searched. He always had enough money available as they approached each checkpoint to buy their way through.

Thomas escorted 27 sleep-deprived, frightened, hungry and thirsty people, including Ed's children and other ACFI members, to Conakry, Guinea. Back in the United States, Ed and Cece waited on their knees for a word from him. Upon arrival to Conakry, Thomas did not know where to go and did not dare ask anyone for assistance in his Liberian English. The Guineans were hostile to anyone who did not speak French, their eyes on Charles Taylor. The weary and precious cargo he carried waited, their eyes on Thomas. The streets were quiet and dark. All his hopes were to make contact with someone from ACFI. He grabbed the nearest pay-phone and called Ed and Cece and told them he reached Conakry. As the report went out from one continent to another, Thomas could hear their rejoicing, singing praises to the Lord! But still Thomas did not know where to go. He felt like Moses, he said. So much responsibility rested on him.

While talking with Ed, he rifled through a phonebook searching for a name he might recognize. A woman approached the same group of pay-phones and took up the one next to him. She glanced Thomas' way and cried out, "Brother Peters! What are you doing here?" Thomas turned and recognized her in amazement and dropped the phonebook. It was Kolu, a woman he knew well from the early days of ACFI. Ed had rented the building from her in Buzzi Quarters which became the clinic and the launching pad for ACFI ministries. She was now living in exile in Conakry.

"Come with me, all of you," she said learning of the others. "Come to my home to eat and rest."

O God, You are my God; I shall seek you earnestly; my soul thirsts for You, my flesh yearns for You in a dry and weary land where there is no water. Thus I have seen You in the sanctuary, to see Your power and Your glory. Because Your lovingkindness is better than life, my lips will praise You. So I will bless You as long as I live; I will lift up my hands in Your name. My soul is satisfied as with marrow and fatness, and my mouth offers praises with joyful lips. When I remember You on my bed, I meditate on You in the night watches, for You have been my help, And in the shadow of Your wings I sing for joy. My soul clings to You; Your right hand upholds me.
(Psalm 63:1-8)

Eventually Ed's weary band of children would have to be moved out of Guinea as anti-Liberian sentiment increased there. One of Ed's sons would have to remain in Guinea, hospitalized for surgical treatment of wounds incurred at the hands of rebels while fleeing Sierra Leone. Finally, Thomas would deliver the others back to Monrovia.

18

In Perils in the City

"God closed they eyeballs, Pappy, because what
they had in mind was evil."

"Once secure in his power, Taylor, like Doe before him,
began purging the government of potential rivals...Taylor
formed a new personal security force, the Anti-Terror Unit
(ATU) to become the primary military organization in the
country" (Lidow 162).

In September of 1998, the ATU invaded Roosevelt Johnson's
headquarters in an attempt to "disarm" him, sparking another
round of violent fighting in Monrovia. Eventually Johnson
would flee to Nigeria. Over the next few months, the ATU
would hunt for Krahn soldiers, civil servants and civilians.
Many fled to refugee camps in the Ivory Coast and Guinea
(Lidow 162). Ed would find himself on Taylor's most wanted list
again and again.

As in previous days of the violent uprisings, hundreds of
people came daily to the ACFI headquarters on the beach to get
relief. The ACFI compound was a focal point of the city. Even
Charles Taylor's ATU soldiers would disguise themselves and
come to receive aid from Ed's hand. They knew Ed's face well.
And Ed, being filled with the Holy Spirit, would not have turned

one away.

He had been careful to remain neutral in all the power plays during the civil war. He knew it was extremely dangerous to be perceived as being loyal to one faction or another. His heart was for the people, especially the most vulnerable. What the Lord deemed as valuable, there lay Ed's allegiance.

He thought that his newly-hired missions director shared in his convictions. He had miscalculated.

Ed recalls being uneasy in his spirit after a day of doling out provisions. The battles raged downtown, a backdrop of pop pop and throaty explosions, grenades detonating, were all unseen but heard from the compound. "The Liberian civilians were hiding out, the streets were deserted, the city a ghost town," Ed recalls.

Were it not for so many years of war, perhaps soft sounds would have been filtering into the evening air, cooks chattering over clanging bowls, women seeking a breeze and visiting with one another on front porches. Monrovia had once been this way, with electricity and infrastructure, running water and people returning home after a day of employment. And food! African food! Food cooked over flames leaving spicy smells to linger in the air instead of sulfur and smoke. And rice! Affordable rice! How they must have longed for those days. There had been too many years of want, and yet an abundance of hatred and violence. The streets of Monrovia seemed to stop singing a song of remembrance. They had sorely submitted to this way of life.

An uneasy Ed asked four of the strong young ACFI men to

walk up the road together with him. He did not want to be alone.

What was unknown to Ed was that his new missions director, who was to have been tending to missions work transporting food and relief supplies in an official ACFI vehicle, had singularly made the decision to stop at the Johnson headquarters and share some supplies during Taylor's campaign to "disarm" his rival. An ATU soldier had witnessed her off-loading food and took note of the ACFI emblem on the side of the van. It was then assumed that Ed and ACFI were sympathizers with Johnson. Reports were relayed and Taylor gave the order to eliminate Ed. ATU soldiers were en route to assassinate him.

Ed and the young men made their way to an upstairs room of a nearby cottage where he had stayed previously with his beloved friend, Wayne Shenk. They stepped outside and onto the balcony listening to gunfire. A group of armed soldiers appeared and then disappeared into an alley in the direction of the ACFI headquarters. Ed assumed they were going to patrol the beach.

After a while, they decided to retire for the night. On his walk toward his home, he reports feeling a heavy sense of dread. However, he took courage and continued. His house faced the main street. There was only one way to enter or exit as, for security reasons, the backdoor had been nailed shut.

What he describes next is astounding. As he entered through the front door, he was suddenly in the presence of ATU soldiers seated in his living room: assault rifles in their hands, ammo garlands strewn over their shoulders, combat boots on the floor. Their eyes locked on him. The two parties faced each other and neither moved. Ed's heart pounded against his ribs. How he must have wanted to turn and run! Run out into the dark! But he stifled the urge and saw that they showed no recognition of him; none. Their muscles remained at rest, their eyes shifted to his companions. Still no movement.

Ed managed a greeting and walked past the seated assassins. His feet carried him into his office where he held onto the desk, head down, breathing thanks to the One who is able to blind the eyes of whomever He wills.

The assault team sat and waited. They did not follow but faced the front door.

Ed fumbled through and grasped some papers while looking back into the room. The women who worked in the house were crouching on the floor, looking most anxious. He knew the only way out was the way he came in. With papers in hand, he headed for the only exit, through the living room again.

When in their presence again, one of the soldiers chastised Ed, "Why do you not speak to people? Why are you in such a way that you just walk back and forth with only a small greeting?" Ed explains that the assassins were voicing their expectation to be treated with the same respect and etiquette as was custom in their country.

"I'm sorry, gentlemen," Ed replied. "I just need a few minutes to do something and I will be right back." He gave them a nod, and they nodded in return. Ed and his companions walked out the front door.

Later, much later, Ed learned from the women who were present in the house that the men had come demanding, "Where is Reverend Kofi?" They responded that he would be back later. Having decided to wait for him, they seated themselves in his living room.

The women witnessed them seeing and talking to Ed. They witnessed them chastising him as he left the building for his lack of manners. They said nothing. After thirty minutes or so had passed, the ATU soldiers started intimidating and harassing the women, "Where is he? Why has he not come?" and accusing them, "You are lying!"

Finally, the boyfriend of one of the women spoke up. "You just saw him. He was just here. You just talked to him, so why are you harassing us?"

They got up and stormed out of the home.

Such peril—such perils in the city—for Ed to have remained among the suffering population in Monrovia feeding anyone who was hungry, even the brutal government soldiers, and then to be hunted by them. Such perils in city politics. This new missions director, had she taken the job to garner support for her favored rebel faction? Had she planned to jeopardize ACFI? Ed still does not know at what point in time she had made an alliance.

Ed once thought that since he was helping the most vulnerable African children he would have been spared. He sadly admits his thinking was wrong.

Soon after, Ed learned of the assassination plot through a fellow believer who worked for the air force. They had developed a relationship years prior when he had approached Ed and asked if he would assist a family member in her endeavors to start a home church. Ed frequented the home church in the city, encouraging them much the way Paul would have done.

This brother overheard Ed Kofi's name in a security briefing after the failed assassination attempt. He learned that Taylor's orders had not been successfully carried out and of the plans to continue pursuing Ed. Not only did he warn Ed, but he also provided an inner room in his very own home for Ed's safekeeping until Ed could make arrangements to leave the area.

Ed breaks out in praise as he tells this story. "Even me, O Lord, even me. It is as though I am reading the very Scriptures themselves."

"God closed they eyeballs, Pappy, because what they had in mind was evil," the women exclaimed who had been crouching on the floor near the assassins.

"This served as a witness to these women," Ed says, "that they would believe."

Ed marvels as well, "How could those who had come to our feeding program over and over not recognize me?" He laughs heartily then sighs and imitates the fooled soldiers, "Where is he! Why has he not come!"

19

In Fastings Often

What does it look like to the Lord when people, who have so little to begin with, fast?

With Charles Taylor elected President the civil unrest continued. Rebel factions with loyalties to Doe, Johnson, and others continued their campaigns for revenge and power. Fathers and mothers were stripped of their dignity. Families starved. Orphans increased in numbers. ACFI continued its mission operating from the beachfront compound donated to the church by Cece's Aunt, Mother Buchanan. Her generosity was in the spirit of the early Church as recorded in the book of Acts when possessions and properties were shared among the body.

ACFI had invested heavily in the compound, shaping it into the ministry center. They worshiped there, they housed pastors and visitors who came to support the mission there, they trained up young leaders in the church there, they spearheaded feeding programs there, they ministered to the blind and Deaf there.

But old women die, and their children can demand what they perceive as their inheritance. In the year 2000, the battle for the ownership of the Oceanview property Mother Buchanan had willed to ACFI was thrust into the courts. The courts ruled in the other relatives' favor. ACFI would have to pay $200,000 to retain the property. All attempts to negotiate failed. Ed called on his fellow servants of the Lord to fast and pray.

This was a fast so that they could continue their ministries from this beloved place, a place given to them on the beaches of their beloved Liberia by a beloved mother in Christ. Where would they have relocated amidst all these years of war and under the corrupt government headed by the warlord, Charles Taylor? How much ground would they lose in service to the poor while they spent energy on relocating and reshaping another property to suit their needs? How much time would go by before people who had been accustomed to coming to these beaches to be fed and taught the Word of God could find them at their new location?

But God...two of the greatest words ever written. *"But God, being rich in mercy, because of His great love with which He loved us, even when we were dead in our transgressions, made us alive together with Christ (by grace you have been saved)" (Eph. 2:4,5). "But as for you, you meant evil against me, but God meant it for good" (Genesis 50:20). "But the* LORD *thy God turned the curse into a blessing" (Deut. 23:5). "And Saul sought David every day, but God delivered him out of his hands" (1 Samuel 23:14). "My flesh and my arm fail, but God is the strength of my heart and my portion forever" (Psalm 73:26). "The nations shall rush like the rushing of many waters; but God shall rebuke them, and they shall flee far off, and shall be chased as the chaff of the mountains before the wind" (Isaiah 17:13).*

But God would move on ACFI's behalf. The hearts of the

relatives would reset, leading them back to the negotiating table with a reasonable offer. ACFI could retain the property for a quarter of the original asking price. This was not insurmountable with the support of the churches from around the globe. The money was raised. The relatives were paid, and today the Oceanview compound is the center of ACFI ministries, including the Liberian Christian College.

Is this not the fast which I choose, to loosen the bonds of wickedness, to undo the bands of the yoke, and to let the oppressed go free and break every yoke? Is it not to divide your bread with the hungry? And bring the homeless poor into the house; when you see the naked, to cover him; and not to hide yourself from your own flesh? Then your light will break out like the dawn, and your recovery will speedily spring forth; and your righteousness will go before you; and the glory of the LORD will be your rear guard.
(Isaiah 58:6-8)

20

In Sleeplessness Often

For in the day of trouble He will conceal me in His tabernacle;
In the secret place of His tent He will hide me...
(Psalm 27:5)

In the year 2000, exiled Liberian politicians formed the Liberians United for Reconciliation and Democracy (LURD) in Guinea, yet another rebel group. Guinea's president increased his support for LURD when Taylor's counter attack of LURD's invasion of Liberia extended into several towns in Guinea. President Conte of Guinea wanted to keep Taylor tied up militarily to prevent future invasions into Guinea (Lidow 163).

By 2002, LURD had succeeded in capturing key cities and large swaths of Liberia. Taylor increased his security forces and started another militia. "By May 2002, intense fighting and extreme levels of civilian abuse resulted in more internally displaced people and refugees" (Lidow 164).

In March, 2003, another insurgency group invaded from Cote d'Ivoire and captured the capital of Grand Gedeh County. This writing does not thoroughly discuss the politics and civil wars erupting in the neighboring countries, but for a better understanding of the increasing intensity of the violence in

Monrovia as well as of Taylor's desperation, a few details must be included. Taylor was squeezed by a United Nations arms embargo leading up to this time, as well (Lidow 164). Taylor held Monrovia, but the insurgents held the ports and much of the country. It became exceedingly difficult to get food.

Ed describes the toxic and tense atmosphere of these years. "The government was suspicious of everyone. Anyone could be a rebel or a spy for the rebels. We were all suspect."

They accused Ed of working undercover for the CIA to oust Taylor. ACFI often brought in western missionaries in support of Operation Save Liberia, whose mission brought the Gospel to Liberians and fed the hungry. Ed feels that government factions also hated his organization for bringing in food to provide for all people in need.

In response to LURD rebels breeching the city limits and gaining ground into a Monrovian suburb, Taylor sent government troops to assassinate Ed. Again he was a wanted man.

Earlier in the day, Ed had been tending to his daily duties. ACFI had moved its orphanage to the suburb of Dixville, a compound of dormitories named the Daniel Hoover village. Housing 500 orphans is a mighty job with many moving parts, as one can imagine. There is both Kingdom work (bringing up the children to know their Savior) and earthly work (providing for their basic needs). On this particular day in June, the septic tanks had overflowed. Ed hired a crew to come and evacuate their contents. While the crew worked, they suddenly heard rockets landing nearby. Gunfire followed. The owners of the truck radioed the driver and reported that rockets were landing in a northwest suburb where many of the workers lived. Ed dismissed them immediately to tend to their families. Sadly, some of the workers were killed on their way home.

Taylor was pinned in. If Monrovia fell, then it meant a certain, violent, public death for him. Any of the insurgent groups would have made his death a long celebration as they seized the capital.

That night, Ed retired to his sleeping quarters back at the ACFI compound. Around midnight four gunmen entered the building where Ed's children were.

"Where is your father?" they hissed at the children, guns pointed at their heads.

Ed was alerted by his children's screams. Fearing that Taylor had once again sent his ATU security officers for him, he slipped out of his bed and cottage and into the church building through a side door.

He entered the same room where Pastor Bruce would have heard the choir of blind men sing in utter abandon. This room would have been where Ed and other pastors read God's Word aloud, just as Ezra the priest had in the days of Nehemiah rebuilding the wall. This room, with its cold cement floors and walls, tin roof and cobalt blue benches was a very special sort of tabernacle. And so Ed lay down in between two rows of benches. He removed his white t-shirt and hid it underneath him to better conceal himself.

The soldiers entered and fanned out into the room, tapping their machetes against the wooden benches.

"Bishop Kofi, Bishop Kofi," they taunted, "we have come for your head."

Ed lay still, helpless with his arms crossed over his chest and his eyes barely open. He could hear them moving up and down the aisles. They overturned benches, row after row, piling some together, still calling for his head.

"Bishop Kofi...Bishop Kofi..."

Ed's children had run to a neighbor's home, and the neighbor made a phone call to the police depot nearby. The police (government police) thought the intruders were rebels, so a squad was dispatched to the ACFI compound to engage them.

As the men continued to hunt for Ed in the sanctuary, they continued overturning benches until one of them stood directly over Ed. Ed looked up at him, certain he was caught, but he reports that the man seemed to look right at him and then past him. He continued overturning the benches without breaking his rhythm. Ed was soon concealed beneath a wooden barricade made by Charles Taylor's own footmen.

The police arrived and so began hours of exchanged gunfire while Ed stayed beneath his newly made fortress. Government troops vs. government troops. There were no rebels present. It was Taylor's newly formed militia vs. his old. The police apprehended one of the soldiers and hauled him into the station for questioning. It was quickly revealed that this was a government fighter. How many times have we seen the LORD of Hosts employ such warfare tactics against Israel's enemies? It happened when Gideon was immersed in battle as recorded in Judges 7; it happened when Saul was leading an army as it is written in 1 Samuel 14:20, "...*every man's sword was against his fellow, and there was very great confusion.*"

Ed stayed beneath the benches all night, in sleeplessness, until morning. When he arose from his hiding place he checked on his children, and, seeing that they were unharmed, he left the compound.

Ed made his way to a place not far from the airport and into hiding. God sent an armed man to escort him back and forth to the compound to check on his children.

On three different occasions the government troops returned to the compound looking for Ed. On the third day, they arrived with a fleet of trucks. They proceeded to loot the compound. Trucks would pull in empty and drive away full. Men, eager to find favor with Charles Taylor, stole from the very hands that had fed them. When they were hungry, members of ACFI did not turn them away. Then, like locusts, they came back in plague formation and swarmed the compound, crawling along its floors and walls, stripping it such that not even the electrical wires were spared. Their intention was ruin and death to the ministry. But they did not know Ed's God. They did not know His Word, for in it He addresses the locusts and has much to say about plagues. Of the locusts, He says through the prophet Joel, "*I will restore to you the years the swarming locust has eaten.*" God would restore the compound. This would not be death to the ministry. As for the plagues, many are yet to come. All are against those who dwell on the earth: the enemies of God's people.

After the time of the locusts, Ed ventured out from hiding

121

and wandered into an open-air market to find some food. He had few possessions. Everything of value to him had been at the compound. He mourned for his study Bible that was full of hand-written notes and precious in his sight. Tucked between its pages, he had stored a government-issued passport, although he had not given the passport any thought.

A man approached him at the market calling to him, "Pappy, Pappy, I know you! I know you, Pappy!" The two men faced each other. "I have your passport, Pappy! I saw a man with your passport pretending to be you. But I know you, so I took it from him." Ed looked at the man and knew he was lying.

"Give me some money," the man demanded, extending his hand.

But Ed's answer was surely not what the man had expected. "I don't want the passport," Ed retorted batting the man's hand down. "What I do, I do for the Most High God. Now, where is my Bible?"

The man produced no Bible. There was no moment of repentance or conversion. He merely shrugged and turned and walked away. Ed was certain, as he stared at the man's back, that he was one of the men who had ransacked the compound. He figures he had stolen the Bible, discarded it, and then kept the passport, perceiving it had value to Ed. Ed never found his Bible. He would soon find out, though, that the government orders to eliminate him were dropped. Charles Taylor himself would call off the manhunt. God tells us in Proverbs 21:1 that *the king's heart is like channels of water in the hand of the LORD; He turns it wherever He will.*

Ed would return to the empty compound, but more than likely, unto sleeplessness still.

> *The LORD is my light and my salvation; whom shall I fear?*
> *The LORD is the defense of my life; whom shall I dread?*
> *When evildoers came upon me to devour my flesh, my adversaries*
> *and my enemies, they stumbled and fell.*
> *Though a host encamp against me, my heart will not fear;*
> *though war rise against me, in spite of this I shall be confident.*
> *One thing I have asked from the LORD, that I shall seek:*
> *that I may dwell in the house of the LORD all the days of my life,*
> *to behold the beauty of the LORD and to meditate in His temple.*
> *For in the day of trouble He will conceal me in his tabernacle,*
> *in the secret place of His tent He will hide me:*
> *He will lift me up on a rock.*
> *And now my head will be lifted up above my enemies around me,*
> *And I will offer in His tent sacrifices with shouts of joy;*
> *I will sing, yes, I will sing praises to the LORD.*
> *(Psalm 27:1-6)*

And what happened at the orphanage at Dixville during this time? The LURD rebels invaded. But God would protect His most vulnerable.

21

In the Orphanage
(2002-2003)

Ed understands the Church better than most. During our last set of interviews, he took notice of a map I had drawn of a portion of West Africa to include countries affected by civil wars, places where Ed had spent time in exile and had planted churches. Ed took the pencil from my hand and erased the lines I had drawn.

"We do not see the lines as you do," he said. "This is all one in our minds."

Suddenly my heart soars to meet the Scriptures, *"For You were slain and purchased for God with Your blood men from every tribe and tongue and people and nation. You have made them to be a kingdom of priests to our God, and they will reign upon the earth" (Revelations 5:9-10).* Ed understands the Church.

ACFI was founded to be a church without borders. That included freely moving from Liberia to Sierra Leone to Ghana to Guinea to Cote d'Ivoire as though they were one. His deep desire today is that this expansion continue farther still.

The beauty of this section of the story is the way God erased the lines between Africa and the U.S. through ACFI. Years ago

Ed came to our church, Fellowship Bible Church of Tacoma, on one of his journeys to gather support for ACFI. There are other churches in the U.S. that are faithfully connected to ACFI, but I am intimately connected with the church body here in Tacoma and know the stories of those who answered yes to Ed's plea for help years ago.

One of our pastors, Bruce Stabbert and his wife BJ have embarked on a deeply connected journey with Ed. God has knitted their hearts together in love and has erased the vast waters of the Atlantic between them.

Bruce and BJ's hearts are now as much African as American. Two of their eight children are Liberian, adopted from the ACFI orphanage. This is the Church. And so let us examine the inner workings of the ACFI orphanage in 2002 when the orphanage was still located at the ACFI beachfront compound, and then in 2003 after the move to the suburb of Dixville. Keep this section in mind when reading the later chapter titled, "In Perils of False Brethren," a written account of undercover reporters, five years later, visiting this same orphanage and weaving together a story of false allegations. Although Ed would suffer tremendously as a result of the false report the work recorded below and the heart of the work of ACFI still goes on today.

Today, however, the adversary to the children is poverty and outbreaks like Ebola. During the Ebola crisis, the ACFI workers relocated the Deaf school children to the orphanage, keeping them all together and quarantined under threat of exposure to the highly-contagious virus. The older children taught the younger children basic math and reading lessons to keep their skills sharp during the time of nationwide school closures. Ed is grateful for such stalwart servants, for what would have become of this generation of youth in the midst of these crises one after another? In 2002-2003 the adversaries were both rebel fighters and government soldiers.

In 2002 as the rebels advanced, everyone knew it was only a matter of time until they reached Monrovia. At this time, the orphanage was still located at the ACFI headquarters near the ocean.

The orphanage headmaster, Pastor Sieh and his wife Francis worked tirelessly and faithfully caring for the children. Pastor Sieh is the same Randolph that journeyed with Thomas Peters through Grand Gedeh County on his way to his post as a new ACFI missionary. He had escaped unharmed in the early years of the war and continued to serve the Lord through ACFI. He and his wife are giants of the faith who remain today as devoted workers in the orphanage. A humble and skilled servant named Munty had been a counselor to the children, devoting himself to service for years. A most kind, gentle and wise man, he related well to the children. It was his gift. When missionaries visited, it was Munty who taught them how to care for war-torn, weary, starving Liberian children.

ACFI and a medical mission team from FBC of Tacoma were providing medical care in a clinic on the ACFI compound grounds. The children were with BJ and her assistant and Munty in a separate building. The visiting missionaries had prepared a craft project of making necklaces out of Fruit Loops and each child held one little baggie with the items needed to make a necklace. The news that there was free food where the children gathered reached those waiting in line for medical care. BJ looked up to see a mob of Liberians rushing the children's area. Munty grabbed a loose door to barricade the opening of the building while guiding the women to hide the food. The Fruit Loops and string, the makings of a near riot, were removed from the area. BJ never forgot this vision of Liberian neediness.

In 2003, ACFI moved the children to Dixville, a campus that would serve as their new orphanage, known as the Daniel Hoover Village. As was discussed in the previous chapter, rebels infiltrated the boundaries of Monrovia. FBC once again partnered with ACFI to bring medical care to the public and care for the orphans, the blind and the Deaf. The Liberian ACFI servants, Munty and others, provided for BJ and her assistant, Jenne to join them and stay in Dixville with the children while the rest of the visiting missionary team set up a medical clinic at the Oceanview compound. Pastor Bruce taught and encouraged ACFI pastors, a shepherd of shepherds. Tucked under Munty's wing, BJ worked side by side with her fellow Liberian servants caring for the orphans, teaching them Bible stories and directing plays. They dressed the children in elaborate costumes made in the U.S., sang praise songs all together, held and hugged the smaller children, and counseled and encouraged the older ones. BJ describes this as a deeply tender time they spent together, knowing that war was coming to these children. "God allowed us, through ACFI, to serve Him by preparing and loving them."

This dusty orphanage, a mere speck on the surface of the

earth amidst a landscape of war was a pearl among grains of vengeance and violence. Beyond its grounds men declared ownership of a nation in the same manner that the woman who stood before King Solomon declared ownership of an infant, willing to have him sawn in two. And yet in the midst of it all stood this treasure, everything that God holds dear: the most vulnerable, and virtues such as faith, love and service. God had sewn these lives together, His hand sweeping stitches back and forth from one side of the world to the other creating a fabric foreshadowing the scene in Revelation of the Church coming together to worship the Lord—from ACFI pastors to American ones, from wise, gentle Liberian servants who spent their lives loving and caring for children to American church members who had the same gift of compassion.

Prior to their trip to Liberia this small team of missionaries carefully weaved together a curriculum to build faith and courage, the makings of armor. The themes were taken from Joseph's life: what man meant for evil, God meant for good. Trust God, for He is good and He sees all that you are going through. Knowing the Liberian kids loved drama, the team created elaborate costumes to act out the story of Daniel: glittering gold helmets, large purple plumes, gold breastplates to fit tiny frames. They taught them songs to belt out such as the children's favorite: Joshua fought the battle of Jericho. They wanted the most vulnerable to feel big and powerful in God's strength like Daniel, Shadrach, Meshach and Abed-nego.

As the rebels swarmed the capital, this small team of missionaries made the very last plane out of Monrovia. The pain of the frantic fleeing was nothing compared to the pain of leaving the children behind.

The final event the missionary team had planned before the evacuation was a treasure hunt. They taught the children that Jesus says where your treasure is, there your heart will be also. The children were not familiar with treasure hunts. The entire medical team came out to the children's village on this last day to assist in this activity. The children were organized into teams. Each team was assigned an adult to assist them in reading and following the clues. As each team discovered the treasure box, they looked inside to find instructions that read, "Your treasure is in your dorm." They raced to their dorms, squealing in anticipation. As they scrambled into their rooms, they found a personalized Bible on every bed, one for every child. Some team members had located an engraving instrument from a Bible book store. They had spent many nights prior to the trip engraving Liberian names onto these leather Bibles. They then carted the used instrument to Liberia to add the names of the new arrivals to the orphanage. Such care.

Every orphan had a Bible with his or her very own name on the cover. They were accustomed to having no personal possessions. Everything is shared in an orphanage. The children cried and cried when they saw their names. Did they cry because they finally possessed something, or because their names were known? Or because they had their own Bible? Maybe for all these reasons. They cried, God continued to weave, and the church grew.

22

In Perils of the Gentiles
(In the orphanage, still)

Pastor Sieh was on site at the Daniel Hoover Village as was his wife and many of the staff members when the LURD rebels invaded in July 2003. The census of the Village was approximately 600 in all: 500 children and 100 staff members. Pastor Sieh explains that when the rebels infiltrated this suburb, they perceived that anyone who stayed behind was doing so in resistance to their invasion. The rebels stumbled onto the compound and found it still populated, to their surprise.

They came upon the scene firing their automatic rifles at the ground and into the air. Pastor Sieh instructed everyone who was outside to take shelter on the floors inside the buildings. The rebels called to them, "Whoever is head of this place, show yourself or we will shoot inside the buildings." Pastor Sieh emerged, hands high in the air, expecting to die for the Truth, he says.

"When I came out, they slapped me and told me to call everyone out or else they would start shooting inside the buildings, so I called the matrons and the children. They came out and the rebels started shooting at the ground in between my legs. The children were crying."

One of the rebels demanded, "What are you doing here?"

"This is an orphanage," Pastor Sieh replied. "We are not being defiant. We just have nowhere else to go."

"They beat the women and the older children and then took me behind the building. They had me place my hands on a rail, and they beat my hands with the butts of their guns." All these years later, he holds out his hand and points to his wedding band cracked clear through. "They fired again in between my feet. My wife and the children could not see me and thought they shot me to death. I could hear them crying." In the height of their abuse, Pastor Sieh explains he thought for certain he would die there, but one of the LURD soldiers suddenly interrupted the violence.

"Forget about him," he said to the others. "This one is my Pappy. Do not kill him. He is my Pappy."

Pastor Sieh explains that that is a term they use meaning "I know him," and "I have high regard for him." The others lowered their weapons.

In the year prior, when the LURD rebels were violently taking over much of Liberia, Pastor Sieh was in another part of Monrovia and was approached by one of these young men dressed as a rebel. He asked if there was any work that Pastor Sieh could give him so that he could earn some money. Pastor Sieh did not hesitate but found work for him fixing a wire fence, and he paid him appropriately. The boy returned the following weeks and, each time, he was given work and paid. He used some of the money to attend a high school for a time. Pastor Sieh had recognized him immediately upon the invasion. He saved Pastor's Sieh's life.

A young woman who was an orphan during the time of the invasion recalls the event. Her name was Handful, but she now goes by the name of Rayna after coming to the U.S. The girls were in their dorms when the rebels came into the compound. She was 13 years old at the time.

"We were in our dorm dressing up and braiding our hair, getting ready for the Independence Day celebration. We were all excited about having chicken and special food. We heard shooting and people yelling, 'They're shooting, they're shooting!' Everyone got quiet to listen to what was going on. Two rebels came into our room and got us into the living room. They were aggressive and pushy, asking us questions like, 'Why are you here? Who is your big boss?' They were yelling at us and grabbing us by the backs of our shirts and dragging us around. They pushed everyone outside. There was a lot of screaming and yelling. One of the matrons fainted.

"Everyone was scared. But the cool part was that we all knew the Lord. That part made me calm. These rebels were just ignorant people doing what they were told. If I died, I knew, this day, I would be with the Lord. But if they died...Some of them got into the food and ate the chicken without cooking it. They were taking our things and making fun of us. They took some of the costume pieces from the plays and put pieces on their heads, making fun, jumping around and being violent and destructive. Some of them started vomiting from the uncooked chicken.

"One of the rebels was trying to protect one of the orphan

girls. He kept trying to protect her from the others. She was his sister.

"We saw them shooting at Pastor Sieh between his legs. They took some of us back inside a building and made us look for money, but we didn't know where any money was. They took us back outside again when they discovered the money.

"They were beating Brother Munty in the yard. They just kept beating him." Rayna pauses in distress as she recalls the brutality of the beating, the blows to the head and face, the blood. This counselor and missionary trainer was the most beloved of the children. She then continues, "In between, he would look at his abusers and say calmly, 'Please, in the Name of God, you must go.' Then they would beat him more. He kept talking calmly to them, 'You don't have to do this. In the Name of God, go.'"

Throughout the years of civil war, so many lives were destroyed in similar scenes where a rebel group descended upon civilians. It was all too common: the girls were assaulted and the young men tortured and murdered. But on this day, the rebel who protected his little sister spoke up and convinced the others to stop, Rayna says. They left the compound shortly after.

Not one life was lost and not one girl assaulted. God took such violent young men in the process of brutalizing and terrorizing, and turned them. He somehow reminded them of a remnant of tenderness, a part of them that had been surely buried deep inside hardened hearts, but not beyond the reach of the Savior of the world.

Before they left, they searched the storage house and found

bicycles that they did not know how to ride. They mounted the bicycles, flopping over again and again while they vomited. They wrestled with the guns strapped to their backs while they wrestled with the handlebars. The children and staff watched them leave the compound in such a manner.

Two days later, a group of Charles Taylor's government soldiers stormed the compound. One of them interrogated Pastor Sieh, "This is a rebel zone, a battle zone. If you are here, we consider you a rebel. If I come back and find you here, I will kill all of you."

Pastor Sieh called Munty, and together they decided to evacuate immediately. This was an exodus of sorts where the 500 children and 100 staff members were taken out of the shelter of their compound and forced to march through the center of Monrovia en route to the ACFI headquarters. The older ones carried the very young. The crying and clinging to one another made this trek a trail of tears. Frances had instructed them before leaving, urging them to leave behind their possessions. They wore their trousers and layered two more shirts atop the one they wore, instructed to carry nothing in their hands as it would only slow them down and make their hands bleed. Pastor Sieh stayed behind and searched the grounds for any children who may have hidden themselves or been left behind. He followed the weeping children from the rear.

The roads had been stripped completely, the blacktop peeled up by government equipment. The terrain had been made into some sort of badlands by the government soldiers' intent on leaving no area laced with conveniences for the rebels to occupy.

They stopped and rested at an old high school. Rayna describes this night as extremely frightening. Sounds echoed through the hollow building, and the children felt as though any one of them could be snatched away in the dark. A dank smell lingered. The children sat on the cold, hard floor, and the matrons doled out the small provisions of food. There was not enough for everyone, so Rayna gave hers away. One night spent in this place was all that Rayna said she could bear.

The following day as the children and staff approached another stopping point along the way to the headquarters, government soldiers came along from the direction of Dixville in a pick-up truck full of goods they had looted from the orphanage. But some of the older boys from the orphanage rallied and surrounded the truck, taking back some bags of rice. As they continued their journey on foot, many lifted their voices in song, marching and singing, "I know the Lord will make a way for me." Pastor Sieh comments, "No one could shoot them for they were covered by so many international prayers."

They arrived at the old school for the Deaf and were soon transported to a walled compound near the Oceanview compound. They stayed there from July through November and then returned home to Dixville. When asked how the children responded after their return—were they more faithful or were they more fearful?—Pastor Sieh gives an honest answer.

"Some trusted God. Some grew in fear."

The government soldiers had looted the orphanage. Nothing

was left. There were no doors, no windows, no beds, no lights. Everything was taken. The children's Bibles were gone, as well.

Friends of ACFI, Wayne Shenk and others came and gathered provisions to restore the village. In August, Charles Taylor had resigned and fled to Nigeria. The weary people of Liberia could now have hope as they tended to the casualties and to rebuilding.

Before the days of the invasions, Rayna recalls being in the choir at the ACFI orphanage and learning worship songs that they all sang during church services. One of the songs was so beloved by the children that they would break out in song during meals, "O sing it! I put my trust in the Lord...I say, I put my trust in the Lord! When trouble comes my way, I put my trust in the Lord!" Sometimes the matrons would bark at the children during mealtime, "Enough! Be quiet!"

During the exodus from the orphanage, Rayna was third in line and carried a small child in her arms. She remembers being terrified that one of the small children would be snatched away. But she also remembers singing. Someone had begun to sing their beloved song and soon many of the children joined in as they walked. "O sing it! I put my trust in the Lord...I say, I put my trust in the Lord! When trouble comes my way, I put my trust in the Lord!"

The Word of God reveals that the Lord inhabits the praises of His people (Psalm 22:3). In one of the greatest battles recorded in 2 Chronicles 20, King Jehoshaphat, when faced with an overwhelming enemy force, seeks the Lord as his deliverer.

"Jehoshaphat was afraid and turned his attention to seek the LORD." He gathered the inhabitants of Judah together and prayed. But it is in his next action that he demonstrates his faith. Instead of aligning for battle in a traditional manner, with his elite fighting forces at the front of the assembly, Jehoshophat stationed the choir at the head. *"He appointed those who sang to the LORD and those who praised Him in holy attire, as they went out before the army and said, 'Give thanks to the LORD, for His lovingkindness is everlasting.' When they began singing and praising, the LORD set ambushes against the sons of Ammon, Moab, and Mount Sier, who had come against Judah; so they were routed."* It was not their battle, Jehoshophat knew, but the Lord's.

At what point in a child's faith walk does he or she come to grasp such confidence in the Lord? It is impressive to say the least that these children sang songs praising the Lord during such a frightening ordeal. It is impressive to say the least that the ACFI orphans were being trained up in the ways of God (whether by permanent staff members or visiting missionaries) amidst the perils of a country collapsing. But this has always been ACFI's mission, and it still is today, that they may know Him. And it is in knowing Him that one can trust Him.

For we are powerless before this great multitude who are coming against us; nor do we know what to do, but our eyes are on You.
(2 Chronicles 20:12)

One final note: The following year, the missionary team from

Tacoma would return with new Bibles and their engraving instrument to replace the ones that the government soldiers had taken.

23

In Perils of False Brethren

Eight years ago, BBC undercover reporters painted T. Edward Kofi as a child trafficker. The network carried the report, and Ed's name and face were smeared across television screens internationally. Donations in support of ACFI plummeted 70%, and to this day, they have not fully recovered. After all he had been through in the wars, this has been perhaps his greatest trial.

An English woman and man came to the Daniel Hoover Village orphanage one day in 2008. The sun was strong and Ed was already heavily immersed in the day's responsibilities. He gladly stopped to engage the visitors. They told him they were seeking information on adoption.

"Good," Ed responded in his Liberian accent. "We are in the business of children here," he said with a laugh. He gestured to the compound behind him: the modest ranch-style dormitories packed with bunk beds against aqua and peach painted walls, the worn basketball goal shooting up from the dirt like a lone sunflower, the center pavilion which offered shade to those gathered for worship, prayer, schooling, performances, and more. Anyone who knows Ed knows he was giving a witty reply to the couple. Hopefully after spending a little time in this writing, the reader has gained a sense of his purpose and heart toward the children.

This couple expressed an interest in partnering with ACFI and giving to the orphanage. Ed believed them. Arrangements were made, and he and Cece met them at a nearby restaurant on a following day.

Ed assumed his heart and lifework were known to these people. And, as can happen to any busy person, he had been distracted when he made the careless comment, "We are in the business of children." *A new couple coming to adopt. Wonderful. Our children need homes and family love. Come on in. We are on the same page. We are on the same team...just a minute while I check my watch as the delivery of rice has been delayed in recent days, and if it does not arrive soon the children won't have anything to eat, and the septic tank needs to be pumped again, and I have been in communication with one of my pastors who is suffering again, he and his family, and there is not enough money to build the Bible college to train up the next generation of pastors which has been my hope for some time, and I must find a way to raise enough funds to pay for a concrete wall to keep looters out of the storehouse since it was just reported to me there was yet another break-in and vital supplies for the children were stolen. (Smiling.)* Come, sit down, my friends. Let me answer your questions and get to know you.

Entire books can be written addressing international adoption: the politics involved and the philosophies that promote and oppose. This is not that book. Ed is very clear where he stands. "What the children have known is a culture of war," he says. "We want them to be raised in loving families in stable communities away from war and famine." His heart is to provide for them. And so Ed is for adoption. Adoption is not trafficking. He never saw this coming.

As Ed and Cece took their seats in the restaurant, they took note of a camera set up nearby. They thought the couple wanted to conduct an interview to promote what ACFI was doing for the children. The "meeting" quickly became a kind of interrogation. Ed patiently endured and openly answered questions. When confronted about a Liberian moratorium on adoptions, Ed appealed to the law. "The laws of the country allow for adoption," he responded, "until the laws are appealed by the legislature. Whatever we do, we do legally." He discussed all matters raised by the undercover reporters. They flooded him with more questions and accusations. He defended and hid nothing. It became apparent that someone had directed the reporters to ACFI. But who would benefit from such slander? Those in competition with ACFI? Perhaps newer adoption agencies attempting to gain a foothold, but even more so, groups who work to persuade governments to discourage adoptions in third world countries would benefit. By putting a face on an anti-adoption campaign, demonizing the ones on the ground providing adoption services, they could eliminate adoptions altogether.

"We are in the business of children."

"We are in the business of children."

This secretly recorded remark as Ed spoke it during the reporters' first visit to the orphanage was smeared all over television screens tuned into the BBC network. The statement was then coupled with the narration that portrayed Ed as fluctuating between child-trafficking and breaking the "new adoption law." It was a publicist's nightmare, if he'd had one, flashes of sunlight reflecting off of Ed's shiny watch, his eyes covered by mirrored sunglasses, his thick forearms gesturing as he spoke through a wide smile. They sarcastically referred to him as charismatic. The network ran the piece over and over again.

Supporters withdrew their support. Westerners caught a whiff of Ed's name and child trafficking allegations spoken in the same sentence and they closed their purses and turned their backs. ACFI financial support dwindled. And Ed suffered. How he has suffered, his name no longer spoken but sneered. His honor, his personal integrity—that which he had built from the time his father had brought him home by the scruff of his neck—was demolished. Such perils of false brethren.

On one of his visits to Liberia after 2008, our pastor preached a sermon to the ACFI pastors on the letter to the Philippians. With Ed's trial on his heart, he was focusing on how God the Father conferred on Jesus Christ the name greater than every name. "Have you ever known someone so misunderstood that you longed to see him vindicated?" he asked.

We read the gospels and see that many did not understand the Son of God and then persecuted Him. His answers to questions were simple yet riveting. His works testified of His identity, and yet He had many adversaries. I am not comparing Ed Kofi to the Son of God, but I am certain that Christ knows intimately of this kind of suffering. He tells us in Hebrews 4:15 that we do not have a high priest who cannot sympathize with our weaknesses, but One who has been tempted in all things as we are, yet without sin.

As our pastor finished his sermon, he turned toward Ed as Ed attempted to slip out the side door, trying to choke back tears. The final words of the sermon: "God will not forget or let you regret the sacrifices you have made for Him."

In chapter thirteen, there was a call to remember how the children came to be gathered into the first ACFI orphanage. Thomas had reported how in 1992, as a result of the years of war there were children everywhere in the streets of Monrovia. The servants of the Lord responded with action. They provided for them. Plain and simple. They did not observe the tragedy of so many orphans and wait for an outside organization to assist. They, themselves, rolled up their sleeves, and the first ACFI orphanage was born. Adoption only made sense to these people who were fighting for life on behalf of the most vulnerable. But it has become fashionable to argue that children must remain in their country of origin. Articulate, impassioned voices cry out against removing them, regardless of their country's or personal perils. Let the debate continue and let us have good reasoning in common. But the slandering of a man's name and potentially demolishing his life work in order to advance one side's agenda must not be allowed to stand. Our sincere hope is that Ed's name is cleared and the work done through ACFI continue and grow. Yes, he is for international adoption. But adoption is not trafficking. Adoption, from many people's point of view, is a loving solution.

*O afflicted one, storm-tossed and not comforted, behold, I will set
your stones in antimony, and lay your foundations with
sapphires. I will make your pinnacles of agate, your gates of
carbuncles, and all your wall of precious stones. All your children
shall be taught by the LORD, and great shall be the peace of your
children. In righteousness you shall be established; you shall be
far from oppression, for you shall not fear; and from terror, for it
shall not come near you. If anyone stirs up strife, it is not from
Me; Whoever stirs up strife with you shall fall because of you.
Behold, I have created the smith who blows the fire of coals
and produces a weapon for its purpose. I have also created the
ravager to destroy; no weapon that is fashioned against you shall
succeed, and you shall refute every tongue that rises against
you in judgment. This is the heritage of the servants of the LORD
and their vindication from Me, declares the LORD.*
(Isaiah 54:11-17)

In Closing

"I am a witness. The joy of the Lord will always abide."
Ed Kofi

Paul speaks repeatedly of the race we members of the body of Christ are called to run. *"Do you not know that in a race all the runners run, but only one receives the prize? So run that you may obtain it"* (1 Corinthians 9:24). And in his last letter to Timothy, *"I have fought the good fight. I have finished the race. I have kept the faith"* (2 Timothy 4:7). In regards to running the good race, Ed tells me of three types of Church members: breastbone, jawbone and backbone members.

The breastbone member stands on the sidelines of the race and beats his breast. He grieves both for those who are running, observing their stress and strain, and for the cause for which they run. "Oh, I am so sorry for all your suffering!" His agony is heartfelt, and the runners can see it in his expression as they pass him by. His only real movement is of his beating his breast.

The jawbone member speaks to the other bystanders regarding the afflicted and the plans to alleviate their suffering. He even speaks of entering the race to those who stop running for a moment to take a drink. He talks at length and in great detail of grand plans and possible roadblocks to such grand plans. But there he stands, at the sidelines. His only real movement is of his jaw.

The backbone member enters the race, and there he remains.

Firm. Steadfast. He remains among those who suffer. He may implement pieces of a Good Samaritan plan, he may slog through roadblocks, he may weep and wail at the end of the day, but what sets him apart is that he endures. He is, according to the book of James, a doer of the Word.

Now I ask you, are you a breastbone, a jawbone or a backbone member?

The purpose of this book is to bear witness to our Lord's saving grace and His relentless pursuit of souls as displayed in the life of Ed Kofi and Ed's devotion to Jesus Christ through ACFI. I pray that you've been emotionally transported to West Africa while reading *Liberian Son* and can "see" these people on the frontlines and those on the ground who turn the wheels of ACFI. Not only will this book serve as a testimony to the church and of these brave servants, but the sales of this book will further support their work.

In recent years, the Ebola crisis hurled Liberia onto the television screens and front pages of newspapers throughout my beloved United States of America. It was not that long ago when, upon mentioning our partnership with a dear brother from Liberia, we would need to explain where Liberia was and what events left it in such a perilous state, namely, the civil war. But then came Ebola. In the midst of the ravaging effects of the deadly virus, God provided through ACFI, despite ACFI's financial state having been crippled by the slanderous report of 2008 regarding international adoption. Ed continued to strive to gather support from churches, send containers of food and medical supplies to the orphanages and minister to the family members who had lost loved ones in the pandemic. He encouraged his pastors, and ACFI continued to bring the news of salvation through Jesus Christ alone to a panicked population. He is still devoting his life to the most vulnerable.

If you are looking to enter the race, enter here. ACFI has a history of loving and serving all people in need. Do not forget how the Lord supplied their needs, time and time again, through the church, whether it was containers filled with food and vital supplies arriving in Freetown, Sierra Leone, or Wayne Shenk, a brother in Christ answering the call to come and bring aid saving Ed's life, or missionaries delivering Bibles into tiny vulnerable hands. Think of the orphans in distress, the contending for the blind and the Deaf, visiting pastors teaching and encouraging their dear Liberian brothers and sisters, abundant food on the beaches of Monrovia sustaining the war-torn refugees, medical teams laboring for the sick, or containers of economically inflated rice arriving during the Ebola crisis. And not only these, but much more so the proclaiming of the truth that Jesus Christ is Lord and died for our sins and now lives, so that we might live through faith in Him. The saving of lives on the earth, the saving of lives for eternity—all supplied by God through His ministering agents: the Church on the global scale. You are the Church. The need now is still great.

As for Ed, he has treasured his time spent with a significant mentor in his life, an elder woman he refers to as Mother Hoover, a doer of the Word. She and her husband lived their lives as steadfast supporters of ACFI all the way from Pennsylvania. They donated 90% of the funds needed to build the orphanage in Dixville. In fact, the orphanage bears Mr. Hoover's name. They became targets of intense criticism when they stood shoulder-to-shoulder with Ed during his toughest years. He describes them as parents to him, and he is most grateful for their love and counsel.

On a visit some years ago, he said to Mrs. Hoover, "Mother Hoover, I think it is time for me to quit now. My life between nations is so difficult, and I am carrying a great load." But Mother Hoover replied, "Edward, our God is not a quitter."

For all he has seen, and all he has heard, and all he has done, Ed's personal desire is to be a pastor of a small church in rural Liberia, his beloved homeland, the wife of his youth with him at all times. But he knows for him that would be quitting. This son of Liberia's concern for the churches compels him to persevere and continue to serve the Most High God in all of West Africa, his eyes set on the entire continent, his hands firmly gripping the vine of the tie-tie tree.

We are afflicted in every way, but not crushed; perplexed, but not despairing; persecuted, but not forsaken; struck down, but not destroyed; always carrying about in the body the dying of Jesus, so that the life of Jesus also may be manifested in our body. For we who live are constantly being delivered over to death for Jesus' sake, so that the life of Jesus also may be manifested in our mortal flesh. So death works in us, but life in you.

(2 Corinthians 4:8-12)

Dr. Ed Kofi

ACFI Beachfront Compound.

Pastor Bruce Stabbert teaches ACFI pastors in the oceanview chapel. This was the same sanctuary where Ed hid from rebels beneath the pews during the civil war.

Buzzi Quarters—the poorest area of Monrovia just beneath the presidential palace, the birthplace of ACFI clinic ministry.

Buzzi Quarters clinic.

Ed Kofi in his office.

ACFI leaders and Ed (kneeling in front of Cece).
Randolph Sieh on the far right.

Thomas Peters and Tukutu.

The Daniel Hoover children's village—an ACFI
orphanage established during the civil war.

Missionary BJ and the orphan children just before
rebels invaded the orphanage.

Children at the Oscar and Viola Stewart ACFI School
for the Deaf receive containers from U.S. churches
during the Ebola crisis.

Ed holds the hand of a small Deaf child, Moses,
who just learned to sign his name.

Liberian ACFI teachers at an annual teaching conference.

Liberians awaiting medical care outside an ACFI-sponsored
clinic during a village medical mission in 2012.

The view from the medical team's bus as they leave Fish
Town after an ACFI-sponsored medical mission and
evangelism meeting.

The author, Joan Brown, interacts with children of Fish
Town at the end of a medical clinic day in 2008.

Team of missionaries serve alongside ACFI in
medical and construction missions.

Physician from the Tacoma, WA, church administers care to mother and child during a 2013 mission trip.

Local children in the town of Saw Mill play near a newly planted ACFI church.

Young ACFI pastor and his wife. Their church in Bomi
County was planted after a medical team delivered care.

ACFI elders and leaders gather for prayer
and communion in 2016.

If you are interested in reading more about or donating to ACFI's ongoing ministries and mission, please refer to their website: **http://www.acfiliberia.org/.**

Bibliography

Bulow, Louis. "Oskar Schindler, rescuer of Jews during the holocaust. http://auschwitz.dk/Schindler2.htm. 1996. 2 Feb. 2015.

Ellis, Stephen. 1999. The Mask of Anarchy: The Destruction of Liberia and the Religious Dimensions of an African Civil War (New York: New York University Press).

Lidow, Nicholai. *Violent Order: Rebel Organization and Liberia's Civil War.* Stanford University, 2011.

Levitt, Jeremy I. 2005. The Evolution of Deadly Conflict in Liberia (Durham: Carolina Academic Press).

Times of London. 1931. "The Liberian Report: Slavery Charge Proved" (11 January).

UNSC (United Nations Security Council). 1996b. "Seventeenth Progress Report of the Secretary-General on the United Nations Observer Mission in Liberia" (S/1996/362).

www.globalwitness.org/campaigns/conflict/post-conflict/liberia-sierra-leone-and-charles-taylor.

Note: All biblical references are taken from the New American Standard Bible.

About the Author

Joan Brown lives in the Pacific Northwest. Joan is married with five children and one grandson. She enjoys writing, painting and studying God's Word.

With *Liberian Son* and her other written works, Joan's hope is that readers are inspired to look to our Father in heaven, to give glory to Him and to offer support to His workers on the ground who serve Him.

Liberian Son is proudly published by:

Creative Force Press

www.CreativeForcePress.com

Do You Have a Book in You?

Made in the USA
Columbia, SC
05 July 2021

41405313R10100